PIVOT

PIVOT

HOW ONE TURN IN ATTITUDE
CAN LEAD TO SUCCESS

DR. ALAN R. ZIMMERMAN

PEAK PERFORMANCE PUBLISHERS

Submit all requests for reprinting to:
Greenleaf Book Group LP
4425 Mopac South, Suite 600
Longhorn Bldg., 3rd Floor
Austin, TX 78735
(512) 891-6100

Published in the United States by Peak Performance Publishers

Composition by Greenleaf Book Group LP
Cover Design by Greenleaf Book Group LP

First Edition
10 9 8 7 6 5 4 3 2

Contents

Introduction

I've been observing people for years. I love to observe people, because I find them so very fascinating. They all look a bit different, and they all have a lesson to teach me.

When I started a successful door-to-door business in the second grade, I watched my customers. Some of them were warm and outgoing, while others were quiet and reserved.

When I started an international import business in the sixth grade, I watched my suppliers. Some of them were fair and honest, while others cared only about themselves.

I watched the inmates when I worked as a counselor in a juvenile reformatory. Some of them wanted to make a new start in life, and others did nothing but blame other people for the problems they had.

I watched my students when I taught at a university. I found little or no correlation between my students' aptitudes and their academic achievements.

Now I've been speaking for various organizations for more than twenty years. I've been in front of thousands and thousands of people, and I'm constantly watching my audience members.

Through all of this observation, I've noticed that attitude makes a huge difference in determining a person's level of success in life. In fact, attitude seems to make a bigger difference than age, sex, race, education, circumstance, or any other factor. Two people can have the same background and face the same situations, but experience very different outcomes. It's all about attitude.

Unfortunately, many people have no idea how important attitude is. They don't realize that their positive or negative attitudes may be making or breaking them on or off the job. They may not even know they have the "wrong" attitudes. They figure that's just the way they are. The first three chapters of this book are for these people. They will learn the importance of a positive attitude, and they will learn how to eliminate a negative attitude.

I've also found many people who know they *should* have a positive attitude, but they have no idea how to get one. They confuse a positive attitude with happiness, thinking if they have the right attitude they'll never have problems or never feel down. And that, of course, is impossible. But positive people possess skills that keep them upbeat and motivated, moving through their problems, achieving their goals, and making the best of any situation. Chapters four through seven tell you how to achieve that kind of positive attitude.

And then there are people who know the importance of a positive attitude and how to get one, but they don't know how to keep their positive attitudes. When worries or failures come along, their positive attitudes fizzle away. Chapters eight and nine tell you how to maintain a positive attitude despite the changes and challenges in your life.

You may be a skeptic. You may think it's almost impossible for you to get and keep a positive attitude. You may think that I don't understand how difficult your parents, spouse, children, finances, health, company, boss, job, coworkers, customers, or whatever are.

I do understand. This positive-attitude thing didn't come easily for me. I grew up in a family that was deeply touched by abuse, alcoholism, imprisonment, and suicide. I've dealt with illness, divorce, and financial strain. Professionally, I've encountered betrayal from coworkers, incompetent direction from bosses, and idiotic change from the executives above. I know what it feels like to have lots of challenges and still maintain a positive attitude.

The information in this book is simple, because I've never been interested in complex, esoteric academic theory. I'm only concerned with what works. The skills in this book work. I've studied, researched, practiced, and lived these skills for years.

But don't let their simplicity fool you. These skills will take work on your part to master. So I encourage you to read and reread the chapters. Practice the skills. Do the exercises. I know you'll be delighted with the successes you'll achieve.

Dr. Alan R. Zimmerman

PART ONE

A Simple Turn

CHAPTER ONE

Awareness

YOUR ATTITUDE DETERMINES YOUR ALTITUDE

The Importance of Attitude

I make my living flying across the country and speaking to all types of groups and all kinds of people. Although I spend a lot of time on airplanes, I seldom take the time to talk to my seatmate. But I'll never forget this one man who sat next to me. He looked terribly down, with drooping shoulders, a sagging face, and eyes that seemed to ask, what's the use?

So I greeted him with a cheerful, "Good to see you. How are you doing?"

He said, "Oh, okay, I guess." We talked for a few minutes and then he asked me, "What do you do for a living?"

I said, "I'm a professional speaker. Some people might call me a motivational speaker. I write books and give presentations on how to be a peak performer."

Then, out of nowhere, he said, "Tell me something. Why does everything go wrong for me?"

Well, I certainly didn't know. I had never met the man. I replied, "Beats me. But if you'll talk to me for a few minutes, perhaps we can figure it out."

For the next thirty minutes he went on and on about all his difficulties. His workload was getting heavier at work, and the management team seemed to change directions every other day. His marriage wasn't the best. His kids pushed their boundaries, and the bills always seemed to exceed the amount of money available to pay them. He repeated the same negative thoughts over and over. He kept saying, "I'll never get ahead. I just can't do it. Nothing ever seems to work out."

Then all of a sudden he exclaimed, "Hold it! Hold it! I know why everything goes wrong for me. It just came to me. Everything goes wrong for me because I'm wrong. I think wrong, speak wrong, and act wrong. I'm just too negative all the time."

He was right. He had gotten right to the crux of the matter: his attitude was determining his altitude.

The same is true for you. Your attitude is one of the most important, most powerful factors in your life. In fact, you can trace just about everything you achieve or don't achieve back to your attitude. Quite simply, good attitudes bring good results, and bad attitudes bring bad results. Your attitude, even more than your aptitude, determines your altitude.

Of course, motivational authors saw the connection between attitude and achievement years ago. James Allen wrote, "Man's rise or fall, success or failure, happiness or unhappiness depends on his attitude." Dr. Norman Vincent Peale said, "Any fact facing us is not as important as our attitude toward it, for that determines our success or failure." Unfortunately, it takes many people a long time to understand this concept.

The Psychological Evidence

Of course, many people think joking about their negative attitude is cool. Comedian W. C. Fields said, "Start every day with a smile and get it over with." One negative person even carried a card in his wallet that read, "In case of accident, I'm not surprised."

Sure, it can be fun to joke about a negative attitude. But in reality, nothing could be more serious. Benjamin Franklin knew that. He said, "Most people die at age eighteen, but we don't bury them until they're sixty-five."

You, on the other hand, may think that all this talk about attitude is just a bunch of fluff. However, there is evidence to back up my claims. The best research comes from Dr. Martin Seligman. In his monumental, groundbreaking book, *Learned Optimism*, Dr. Seligman discovered that attitude was a better predictor of success than IQ, grade point average, or almost any other factor.

He found that negative people get sick more often, are divorced more frequently, and raise kids who get in more trouble. He found that negative people even make less money.

In one long-term study of 1,500 people, 83 percent of the people (group A) chose their particular jobs because they believed they could make lots of money. Only 17 percent of them (group B) chose their jobs because they had positive attitudes towards those jobs.

Twenty years later, the two groups had produced 101 millionaires. The amazing thing is, only one of those millionaires came from group A. One hundred of them came from group B. Now that's significant.

Even more amazing, more than 70 percent of these millionaires never went to college. And more than 70 percent of those who became CEOs graduated in the bottom half of their class. Seligman concluded that their attitudes, rather than their aptitudes, had determined their altitudes. In no uncertain terms, he says positive thinking is *the* hallmark of successful people.

I find similar trends in all the audiences and organizations where I speak and consult. I always ask members of my audience to list the words they would use to characterize a winner, and I write down the first ten they give me.

What do you think they say? Regardless of the group, the answers are always consistent. They list attitude, enthusiasm, determination, motivation, confidence, optimism, dedication, happiness, balance, and patience. What's interesting is that none of these qualities has anything to do with physical or mental ability. But they all relate to attitude in some way or other.

The Medical Evidence

Your attitude can also affect your physical health. Dr. Thomas Hackett, a Harvard psychiatrist, found that sick people who minimize the seriousness of their condition by emphasizing their optimism, hope, trust, and humor have higher survival rates than chronic worriers. He said, "Sometimes the best medicine is in your head . . . a positive attitude has a lifesaving effect."

Leo Goldberger, professor of psychiatry at New York University, said, "We used to think of mind and body as two separate realms when, in effect, they are part and parcel of the same whole."

Grace Murphy of the International Center for the Disabled in New York City wrote, "In order to have a healthy body, you must have a healthy mind."

But Norman Cousins was one of the first to popularize the mind-body connection. As a respected journalist and professor, he wrote and spoke on the topic many times. One particularly interesting study that Cousins reported was conducted on forty patients who recovered from "irreversible" illnesses.

When these patients were told they didn't have much of a chance to survive, they all panicked. That was to be expected.

But at some point each of them decided to reject the notion of inevitable death and live. They took advantage of the best care that medical science had to offer, and they also became actively involved in their own recoveries. They decided to do whatever it took to regain their health. According to Cousins, their decisions to fight death and maintain positive attitudes made the difference in their physical health.

Attitudes have a definite biochemical effect on the body. An attitude of defeat or panic constricts the blood vessels and has a debilitating effect on the entire endocrine system. By contrast, an attitude of confidence and determination activates benevolent, therapeutic secretions in the brain.

Apparently a positive attitude can help in the prevention of disease and also in the recovery from disease. Dr. James Strain, the director of Behavioral Medicine and Consultation Psychiatry at Mount Sinai Hospital in New York City, found this to be true when he compared pessimistic and optimistic men who had had heart attacks. In the first group of twenty-five pessimists, twenty-one died within eight years of a heart attack. Only six of the twenty-five optimistic men died in that time.

Attitudes can even impact the length of your life. In an Oxford, Ohio, study in 1975, a group of 660 people over the age of fifty were asked a series of questions—questions that got at their attitudes toward aging. They were asked whether they agreed or disagreed with statements such as "Things keep getting worse as I get older," "I have as much pep as I did last year," and "I am as happy now as I was when I was younger."

Researchers checked to see which survey respondents were still alive in 1998, and they noted when the others had died. It turned out that those who viewed aging as a positive experience lived, on average, 7.5 years longer than those who took a darker view.

Mary Duenwald of the *New York Times* News Service reported that, according to an Oxford study, a positive outlook on aging provides an advantage far greater than what can be gained from lowering blood pressure or reducing cholesterol, each of which can add four years to your life. It also beats exercise, quitting smoking, and maintaining a healthy weight, strategies that add only one to three years.

I'm not a physician. But I have the privilege of working with some of the finest doctors in the world when I do programs for such organizations as the Kettering Medical Center and the Mayo Clinic. My programs focus on the mind, and the medical doctors focus more on the body, but we both see the definite connection between the two: your attitudes affect your health.

The Difference

More often than not, your attitude is the number one determining factor in your success. With the right attitude, you're almost certain to achieve your goals. And the good news is that your attitude is self-chosen. Ultimately, you're responsible for changing your attitude if it's not as positive or powerful as it needs to be. No one gave you your attitude, and no one can take it away—except you. Your attitude is your responsibility. You control whether or not you will succeed in life, regardless of your natural ability. So you can be a winner. You can have a stronger body, form better relationships, and make more money—if you have the right attitude.

I'm sure you want to be a winner. After all, no one wants to be a loser. And the difference between the two is huge:

- The winner is always a part of the answer. The loser is always a part of the problem.

- The winner always has a program. The loser always has an excuse.
- The winner says, "Let me help you." The loser says, "That's not my job."
- The winner sees an answer for every problem. The loser sees a problem in every answer.
- The winner sees a green near every sand trap. The loser sees a sand trap near every green.
- The winner says, "It may be difficult, but it's possible." The loser says, "It may be possible, but it's too difficult."

I can't think of a bigger winner than Abraham Lincoln. But I also can't think of anyone who was under more pressure in his life or in his career. Whether the pressure was coming from his repeated losses in various elections, his difficult marriage, or the nation falling apart, he lived and led with an indomitable positive attitude. He simply chose to think that way. As he said himself, "Most people are about as happy as they make up their minds to be."

Starting today, make up your mind to be a Lincoln!

AWARENESS EXERCISES

1. Become a Detective

a. Look for information that talks about the importance and impact of attitude. Look for articles in the newspaper, in magazines, in professional journals, or on the Internet. Listen to people when they talk about their successes and how their attitudes played a part in their successes.

b. Does your research tend to confirm or dispute the importance of a positive attitude?

c. What conclusions can you draw from the information you gather?

2. Look at Yourself

a. Spend a few minutes thinking about your own attitudes—in particular, when they are positive and when they are negative.

b. Think about how your behavior and your feelings are influenced by your attitudes. Do you do a better job when your attitudes are positive or negative? Do you feel better physically when your attitudes are positive or negative?

c. Over the course of your lifetime, would you say your attitudes have helped or hurt you? In your career? Your health? Your wealth? Your relationships? Have they affected anything else that is important to you?

CHAPTER TWO

Understanding

YOUR ATTITUDE WILL DEFEAT YOU FASTER THAN ANY PROBLEM YOU WILL EVER HAVE

Good attitudes bring good results, and bad attitudes bring bad results. It's that simple.

Unfortunately, bad attitudes are all too pervasive. According to psychologist Terry Paulson, most people maintain an internal dialogue that is 80 percent negative. That means almost all their thoughts are negative.

Of course, you can easily understand why negative attitudes are so common. Just look at society. The media feeds us a constant diet of negativity.

The news coverage, for example, is 90 percent negative. Only 10 percent of the stories have a humorous or human interest slant. And if the networks don't have enough bad news on a particular day, they replay old video clips on the anniversaries of certain disasters. Perhaps we should rename CNN and call it "Constant Negative News."

The Success Blocker

What's the result of all this negativity? We end up with millions of people who never come close to using their full potential. And we end up with millions of people who spend more time tearing themselves down than they do building themselves up. Unfortunately, very few people are fully aware of the negativity in their lives. Most have no idea how much damage they do to themselves. And most don't realize that they may be their own worst enemies.

That's because negativity comes in several forms. It's more than gloom and doom or griping and groaning. Let me explain by outlining the ways negativity may have infiltrated your life and may be getting in the way of your success. After all, since you're reading this book, I know you want to win. I know you want to achieve your goals. But you won't be able to do that with a negative attitude.

1. EXCUSES, EXCUSES

One way you may be sabotaging yourself is by making excuses. On the surface, your excuses might sound perfectly reasonable, even justifiable. But excuses are nothing more than roadblocks to your success. Someone who is good at making excuses is seldom good for anything else.

Are you ever guilty of saying such things as, "I'm just too fat . . . or too old . . . or too small . . . or my metabolism is too slow for me to ever lose any weight"? Do you ever think, "I just don't have the experience to be successful . . . or get that job . . . or achieve my income goals"? If so, be careful. Excuses are like noses: we all have one, and they all smell.

The difference between winners and losers is the way they view their circumstances. Losers use their circumstances as an *excuse* to give up—while winners use their circumstances as a *reason* to get going. And that's why some people become winners and other people become losers in the same situation. Some people make excuses, while others do not.

Walt Disney used his circumstances as a reason to work harder. As a young boy, Walt was a dreamer. He loved to dwell in the world of fantasy, entertainment, and cartoon. But his success as a cartoonist didn't come instantly; it took determination.

When he first approached a Kansas City newspaper with his drawings, the editor curtly replied, "These won't do. If I were you, I'd give up this work. From these sketches, it's obvious your talent lies elsewhere."

But Walt was determined. His desire to be a cartoonist was strong, and he believed he could do it in spite of the editor's negative appraisal. Walt went to other newspapers, and received rejection after rejection. Still he persevered. He kept knocking on doors until finally he got a job drawing publicity material for churches.

Then Walt began searching for a studio. All he could find was an old mouse-infested garage, but in that garage studio Walt continued to draw and write. From that determined beginning, Walt— and one of the mice—eventually became world famous.

Walt could easily have developed a negative attitude. He could easily have made excuses for not pursuing his dream to be a cartoonist. And he could easily have ended up nowhere. But Walt knew that someone who is good at making excuses is seldom good for anything else.

What about you? Do you have more excuses than determination? Do you tell yourself that you'll be happier when you get a big raise or a better house? Do you think your marriage will improve when your spouse learns how to communicate? Do you think you'll have less stress when the economy improves? Do you wait for things to change before you do? If so, then you're in trouble.

Are you filled with determination? Are you continuously fired up? Are you achieving all that you are capable of achieving? If not, you can change. You can learn to have a positive attitude, and you can nurture your determination.

2. FEAR AND MORE FEAR

A second way that you may be sabotaging yourself is through fear. Negative attitudes show up as the fear of failure, and that fear may stop you from accomplishing all you could accomplish. For example, a salesperson may be afraid of prospecting, so his sales numbers never improve and his career stands still. Businesspeople may be afraid of new information technologies, so their products and services eventually become obsolete. Author John Gardner said, "One of the reasons mature people stop learning is that they become less and less willing to risk failure."

On the personal front, you may be afraid of never being able to accomplish your physical fitness goals, so you wonder why you should bother to start in the first place. You may even fear someday waking up, glancing in the mirror, and looking like the bad photo on your driver's license.

Of course, some of your fears are normal and healthy. They point out the dangers in life. They protect you from harm. But too many people are saddled with abnormal fear that stops them from living a full life or having a productive career.

Abnormal fear is strong. You can feel it grip your stomach and make your heart race. I suppose that's why Paranoids Anonymous won't tell you where they meet! Just teasing. But this kind of fear takes over too much of your life. As someone once said, "Why should I waste my time reliving the past when I can spend it worrying about the future?"

Abnormal fear also prohibits action. It stops people from trying. It encourages people to make excuses rather than making progress.

Unfortunately, I see people with abnormal fears all the time in my audiences. I know unequivocally that they can overcome their fears using the techniques I present. After all, I've read letters and taken calls from hundreds of people over the years. Their success stories go on and on.

But I also know that many people in my audiences don't use the techniques and strategies I teach. They don't even try, because they're afraid. Oh, sure, they get excited by what I share. They get a glimpse of new possibilities, but then they sabotage themselves with fear. They're afraid they might fail if they try a new approach to communication, management, or any number of things. As Shakespeare wrote, "Our fears do make us fail to try and gain the heights that are possible for us."

Motivational researcher Napoleon Hill wondered how many times a person would actually try, on average, before giving up on a new goal. The answer was less than one. Lots of people quit before they even try.

Being saddled with fear is a sad state, especially when fear doesn't have to rule your life. You have a choice. You can acquiesce and let fear dominate your life, or you can dominate your fears. I assume you want the latter.

3. PAIN AVOIDANCE

A third way a negative attitude can creep into your life is through the intense desire to avoid pain. You might fool yourself into thinking that a particular goal would be too hard to achieve, that it would take too much work, and that it just wouldn't be worth it. In reality, such thinking is nothing more than a "rational" attempt to avoid pain. Deep inside, you may not actually want to do what you'd have to do to accomplish your goals. After all, it may hurt.

You've heard the old slogan, "No pain, no gain." Well, that's absolutely true. And because most people don't want to go through the pain, they give up on their goals instead.

This fear of pain explains why most people never achieve true physical fitness. They whimper that losing weight is too hard. David Ulrich makes this tendency clear in his book *Human Resource Champions*. He asks, what percentage of people stop smoking and never start again? Seventeen percent. What percentage of people on Weight Watchers reach their target weight? Five percent. And what percentage of people maintain their target weight? One-half to one percent.

His point is obvious. People often refuse to do the things they have to do to get the results they want. Once again, negative attitudes block success.

What about you? Are you stuck in your old ways, refusing to do what you need to do? Do you put things off instead of doing them immediately? Are you more like the negative folks who think it's too hard? Or are you more like the positive folks who know that things worth having are worth the effort?

Sometimes you have to do things you don't want to do. You may have to work out, day after day, whether you want to or not, if you're going to build the body you desire. And you have to eat the right foods on a regular basis if you're going to have the health you want.

Saint Augustine struggled with pain avoidance. Even though he was one of the greatest theologians of all time, he didn't start out as a saint. He had his own chapter of shameful living filled with wine, women, and song. He knew he was wrong and he knew he should change, but his desire to avoid pain often prevailed. He would say, "Lord, make me pure." Then his nerve would fail, and he would add, "But not now."

Many people are like that. They know they should change, and they know those changes will create something far better than what they presently have. But they don't want to go through the pain and discomfort required to get there. So they delay. Or they fool themselves into thinking that someday they'll actually do the things they hate to create the things they love. They're like the old saying, "He was going to be all a mortal should be, tomorrow. All that he left when living was through was a mountain of things he intended to do."

4. BAD HABITS

Negative attitudes also come out in bad habits. You might think your silly old habit merely gets in the way of your success from time to time. Or you might be well aware of the fact that a major bad habit is choking off your future. Either way, bad habits are simply another form of negativity.

Take Silent Sam, for example. Unlike other children, Sam never made a sound the first few years of his life. As a baby and then as a toddler, he never made the normal "ga-ga" sounds or even attempted to form a word. His parents were naturally quite concerned, so they took him to several doctors to have him examined. The doctors said there was nothing physically wrong with Sam. He just had no desire to speak.

The family got used to this and nicknamed their son "Silent Sam." One morning when Silent Sam was eating breakfast, he opened his mouth and uttered his first sentence. He said, "This oatmeal is darned lumpy."

His parents were shocked, and they asked the obvious question, "After all these years, why do you finally choose to speak?"

Sam said, "Until now, everything has been okay."

Of course, that's just a whimsical story, but it illustrates the fact that getting stuck in a bad habit is easy, and it often takes a long time to get out.

That's because bad habits are the sneakiest little monsters around. You don't notice them until they've taken control. As Dr. Denis Waitley wrote in his book *The Joy of Working*, "Habits start as harmless thoughts. They are like flimsy cobwebs with little substance. Then, with practice, they grow, thought upon thought, fused with self-talk and attitude until they become like steel cables."

Bad habits start with a toehold in your thoughts, move on to a foothold in your behavior, and eventually occupy your entire personality. If you're going to take control of your life, you must break your bad habits before they break you. And it will be a battle. Your habits will defend themselves to the death—either theirs or yours, whichever comes first.

The good news, however, is that you *can* break bad habits. You can replace them with new habits and positive attitudes.

5. LACK OF GOALS

Negative attitudes may also prevent you from setting goals. And that's bad. As the Olympic athletes well know, without goals, they don't have a chance of getting the gold.

What about you? Are you a goal setter? Or are you guilty of winging it?

Most people are guilty of winging it. Some psychologists have estimated that only 3 percent of people get serious enough about their goals to think about them, refine them, and write them out. In fact, the average person spends more time planning a summer vacation than planning his or her life, which is tragic. But that's what a negative attitude can do. It can stop you from setting your goals.

That's tragic because of the clear connection between setting goals and higher achievement. You might notice this phenomenon by actually writing out New Year's resolutions. Though the list itself may be lost, if you found it two or three years later, you would be surprised at how many of your New Year's goals you had accomplished.

The acts of writing out your goals and accomplishing more of them also connect. The act of writing tells your subconscious mind that of all the things in this world, here's a list of the things you want. That gives your mind some focus, and it goes to work on getting them.

But if you have a negative attitude, it may show up in your lack of goals. And your lack of goals will lead to a lack of discipline as well. For example, getting up at 5 a.m. is pure drudgery to many people. So they don't do it. But a goal gives you a what and a why. A goal gets you to set your alarm for 5 a.m., and motivates you to get out of bed and into the gym for your morning exercise.

It gets worse. Without goals, you'll also lack wisdom. In other words, you'll spend too much time on activities that are tension relieving instead of goal achieving. You'll spend your time doing what comes "naturally," doing what's easy or feels good. But that's not how you achieve success.

If you want to be wildly successful, you have to get rid of negative attitudes, and you have to set goals. As fitness coach Kate Larsen says, "Every choice takes you closer to or further from your goal. Where did your choices take you today?"

A Final Thought

Most people simply endure life. They have a few vague dreams, but they're convinced they'll never achieve it. They have jobs they don't like, but they don't do anything about it. And they're frustrated because they feel they didn't get the right breaks in life.

In reality, people don't fail because they don't get the right breaks. People fail because they don't think the thoughts and do the things that will change their circumstances.

You don't have to be like most people. You know how dangerous negative attitudes can be. And now you know how those negative attitudes may be affecting you and your life. So now it's time to take charge and get rid of any negative attitudes you might have. In the following chapters, you'll learn how.

UNDERSTANDING EXERCISES

1. Examine Your Reactions

a. Identify two people who have disappointed, hurt, or angered you. If possible, select two people toward whom you still have some bitterness.

b. Ask yourself, how does my bitterness serve me? Am I happier holding on to it? Do I sleep better? Is my life richer, fuller, and better because of my bitterness?

c. If you find that your bitterness is hurting you, make a decision. Decide to let it go. Walk away from the disappointment—meaning you no longer dwell on it or talk about it. Period!

2. Test Yourself

Answer these questions as honestly as possible. Use the following scale:

5   Always
4   Usually

3   Sometimes
2   Rarely
1   Never

1. When you are forced to change your plans, do you quickly see some advantage in the new situation?

2. When someone is staring at you, do you think it's because he or she finds you attractive?

3. Do you like most of the people you meet?

4. When you think about next year, do you think you'll be better off than you are now?

5. Do you stop to admire things of beauty?

6. When someone finds fault with you or something you've done at work, can you tell the difference between "useful criticism" and "professional jealousy," which is better ignored?

7. Do you praise your spouse, partner, or best friend more than you criticize him or her?

8. Do you believe the human race will survive and thrive for years to come?

9. Are you surprised when a friend lets you down?

10. Do you think of yourself as happy?

11. If you were served a substandard meal in a restaurant, would you ask for it to be replaced?

12. Do you feel comfortable joking about yourself?

13. Do you believe that your state of mind has a positive effect on your physical health?

14. If you made a list of your ten favorite people, would you be on it?

15. When you reflect upon the past few months, do you focus on your successes more than your failures?

Scoring:

68–75	Excellent	You're a powerful positive thinker. Your optimism serves as a driving force as well as a healing influence in your life.
62–67	Very Good	You're a positive thinker most of the time, and your life is much better as a result.
56–61	Good	You're a positive thinker some of the time and you have a foundation on which to build.
50–55	Fair	Your positive and negative thinking patterns are about evenly matched, and as a result, you are stifling some of your natural energy and enthusiasm.
49–15	Poor	You definitely need improvement in your thinking patterns. Your negativity is getting in the way of your success.

CHAPTER THREE

Negativity

YOU HAVE TO CHOOSE TO RISE AND SHINE OR RISE AND WHINE

Every morning you get to choose to rise and shine or rise and whine. That's right: You are responsible for your attitude. So if you go through life with a negative attitude, somehow or other, you chose that outlook. In other words, you chose to rise and whine.

But you can make new choices. You can choose to kill off your negative attitude. Of course, that isn't always easy. You must be prepared for your mind to resist. Your mind will even try to deceive you by saying your old negative attitudes won't go away and your attempts to kill off the negative attitudes won't really work.

When that happens, just remember the saying, "You cannot prevent the birds from flying over your head, but you can keep them from building nests in your hair." In other words, you may not be able to prevent all negative thoughts from coming your way, but you can keep yourself from hanging on to them. And every time you renounce a negative thought, it grows weaker until it is eventually killed off.

If you practice the following eight easy exercises, you can get rid of any negative attitudes you might have. The exercises are simple, even fun, and they work. But you must do them, because you cannot develop and maintain a positive attitude if you are a slave to your old negative attitudes. So let's get started.

1. Identify Your Recurrent Negative Thoughts

After all, a negative attitude is nothing more than a negative thought—thought over and over again. So listen to yourself for four or five days. Don't try to change anything; just observe the negative thoughts that come to mind.

You may find yourself thinking, "I'm too old to do that anymore," "I'm such a jerk," "I'll never get ahead," "I just can't lose any weight," or "I'm no good at selling." If you have a negative attitude, you'll probably end up with a list of ten to twenty phrases that you tell yourself over and over again.

2. Critique Your Negative Thoughts

Write down your most recurrent negative thoughts. Put each thought on a separate index card, and then write out the good and bad aspects of each one. Jot down the pros and cons.

For example, you may have a negative thought pattern about money and your future financial success. So you may write down, "I'll never have any money, and I'll never get ahead."

Then consider the advantages of such a thought, and write them down. You may write, "If I don't expect myself to succeed, I won't be as disappointed when I fail." Write down any advantages that come to mind.

Next outline the disadvantages of having such a negative thought about money, and write them down. You may write, "Depression—I just don't feel good thinking things will never get better." You may also write, "Bitterness—I'm bitter about the fact that everyone around me seems to be making more money than I am," or "Laziness—I figure why bother to knock myself out trying to get ahead when I know it won't do any good anyway." Keep at it until you've captured and written down every possible disadvantage.

Now compare your lists. Almost always, you'll have more disadvantages on your card than advantages. In fact, you probably won't find anything good about your negative thoughts.

Finally, read your cards whenever you find yourself dwelling on one of those old, debilitating negative thoughts. Your list of dislikes or disadvantages will help you discard your negative thoughts.

3. Stop Your Negative Thoughts

Your mind is like a garden. And like a garden, you know that whatever you put into the ground has a good chance of coming up and taking over. One zucchini seed can turn into a plant that occupies your entire garden. And one negative thought, planted in your mind fifty years ago, may still be controlling you today.

For example, maybe you had an elementary teacher who told you that you couldn't sing. In fact, when they had the school sing-along, the teacher told you to simply mouth the words and blend into the background. And now as an adult, you still feel incapable of singing or even trying to sing.

Do you have some negative thoughts planted in your mind? And are you continuing to let additional negative thoughts get into your mind? If so, you've got to stop them. As the old saying goes, "Garbage in, garbage out."

You need to do two things. First, *block the negative thoughts* from getting into your mind.

Think about it. What are the sources of negativity in your life? How can you avoid those effects? Who are the most negative people in your life? Which people create the biggest drag on your enthusiasm? You may have to avoid those people or reduce your exposure to them. You may need to limit your exposure to the news. Most of the news is negative, and very little in the news will inspire you or make your life better.

Identify the negative influences in your life. Pull away from them. Otherwise those negative influences will plant themselves in your mind. That's a given. And you will have to work all that much harder to become the positive person you want to become.

Second, *stop the negative thoughts* that come back to mind. You have to think, say, or act out the word "stop" before the thought has time to develop.

For example, you may have a habit of telling yourself that you're just not smart enough. As soon as the thought comes to mind, think "stop!" You may have to do it ten or twenty times, but it will eventually work. The thought will leave you.

If thinking "stop" doesn't work fast enough or last long enough, try saying "stop" out loud. That's right, shout it out. Say it firmly and confidently. Let your negative thought know you're the boss. And notice how well the technique works for you.

If you still struggle with the same recurring negative thought, use the hand signal for "stop." Pretend you're a traffic cop and put up your hand. This authoritative gesture can put an end to your negative thought. You can even say the word "stop" and act it out at the same time.

Stopping your negative thoughts is a major step in the process of taking control of your mind. Try these three "stopping" exercises. You'll probably find that one of them works better for you than another, and that's fine. But keep using it; you'll master the skill and eliminate the negative thoughts that lead to your negative attitudes.

4. Refuse to Verbalize the Negative

If you're like most people, you probably have one or more vicious cycles operating inside of you. In essence, if you think negatively, you speak negatively. And if you speak negatively, you create a negative attitude that pushes you towards negative behavior.

Some people, for example, say they can't help the way they are, that they just have their bad habits. Does that sound like you?

Well, you can't talk that way. You can't go on and on, talking about your bad habits. In fact, you should drop the word *habit* from your vocabulary, or at least use it sparingly. The words you use are strongly connected to the behaviors you exhibit. When you talk about your bad habits, you're empowering them. You're saying you can't stop yourself from doing certain things. Yes, you can! But the more you talk that way, the more entrenched your negative attitudes and bad habits become. So be very cautious about verbalizing the negative.

For example, instead of saying, "It's going to be a bad day," don't say anything at all about the upcoming day. Or say something positive, such as, "It's going to be a wonderful day." Either way, you predict the future. You set up a self-fulfilling prophecy, so you might as well err on the side of the positive.

Instead of saying, "There's no way I can pay these bills," say, "I'll find a way to get through this." Instead of saying, "I'll never be in shape," say, "I can get in shape." Stay away from verbalizing the negative.

And make an effort to verbalize more of the positive. This technique conditions your mind to be more positive. By using it, you take control of your thoughts, rather than allowing them to control you. And you affirm that great line from William Ernest

Henley's poem, *Invictus*: "I am the master of my fate; I am the captain of my soul."

5. Visualize the Positive

Whenever you find yourself thinking a negative thought, create a positive image to replace it. Negative people, for example, often see themselves as tired, worn out, or a bit lethargic. They may even talk about the fact that they don't have the energy they used to have. But this is the wrong image. If those same folks imagined themselves as being filled with energy, the results would be very different. They would actually feel more energetic and a lot less lethargic. Visualization simply works that way.

Or let's take another example. If you find yourself thinking about a possible upcoming failure, change your picture—immediately. Imagine your success in that situation. And hold that positive picture in your mind until you retrain your thinking.

The great business leaders of today used this strategy yesterday. Even as they worked from card tables in their garages, they pictured themselves walking around their new corporate headquarters. Whenever hints of negativity crept into their minds, they pictured themselves as successful. They retrained their minds, got rid of their negative pictures, and ended up being very successful.

Great athletes do the same thing. A truly fine basketball player will picture the ball going through the hoop every time he takes a shot. Similarly, the top PGA golfers will picture the ball going straight down the fairway. They visualize success, over and over again.

If positive visualization works for those folks, it will also work for you. It will kill off your negative, "can't be done" attitude as it creates a new, more positive direction for your mind to follow.

You may have the bad habit of worrying, for example. And worry is nothing more than negative goal setting or negative visualization. Your worry may be stopping you from doing the good things you need to be doing. That's what happened to one of my audience members, until he learned how to visualize. He sent me the following e-mail:

> A month ago I was employed by a large corporation. I had a good job with a steady income. Everything was going smoothly. In fact, I have to admit I had become rather complacent. Then the roof fell in.
>
> Because of the economy, my company was forced to lay me off. I panicked. I was overwhelmed by a negative attitude. How would I pay my bills or feed my family? It was frightening. I felt like a failure. I worried and worried for days on end, too paralyzed to do anything.
>
> Then I remembered what you said about visualizing. I began to visualize myself as a successful businessperson. I pictured myself doing all the things I would need to do if I were to be successful.
>
> From there I lined up interviews with every company I could find. I read the want ads. I followed up every lead.
>
> Two weeks later I found a better job than the one I'd lost. I got a job with a better salary, more opportunity, and more challenge.
>
> Thank you. You showed me how to kill off the worry by using positive visualization. It worked, and I've gotten on with my life.

Think about the pictures going through your mind. Do you have too many negative pictures? If so, then it's time to replace those pictures with positive visualization.

6. Avoid Slippery Places

If you're honest with yourself, you know that in certain places and situations you are more likely to be negative. These situations are "slippery places" because they cause you to slip away from a positive attitude into a pit of negativity. You must avoid those places and situations whenever possible.

For example, the employee lounge or lunchroom is often known as an extremely negative place in many organizations. People sit around griping about what's wrong with the boss, the company, the customers, the nation, or any other issue. And if you're like most people, throwing in your two cents' worth is easy. In fact, you may find it a lot easier to join in the negativity than talk about the good that is going on.

If the lounge or lunchroom is a slippery place for you, stay away from it. Or pull away if and when the negativity starts. Say something like, "I don't want to be rude, but I have to leave. I just can't listen to a lot of negativity today. I need to be at my best, and negative talk just brings me down."

When you stay away from those people who always talk negatively, you kill off your negative attitude by starving it to death. You deprive it of the very fuel that keeps it going.

7. Do the Opposite

If your negative attitude pushes you to do something, do the opposite. Do the opposite over and over and over again, until you replace your negative habit with a positive one. That's how an acquaintance of mine defeated his bad habit of making unkind remarks about other people.

One day he made an especially nasty remark to his wife concerning a business associate. His wife decided that she couldn't take his meanness any longer, and in no uncertain terms she told him what she thought about his terrible habit.

Fortunately, he took her lecture to heart and decided to get rid of his bad habit. He began doing the opposite of what he used to do. He sought out people with positive attitudes and avoided conversations in which others were being put down. Whenever he was tempted to say something mean, he consciously stopped himself. Instead, he looked for something kind he could say about the person.

It didn't take long before people began to notice a change in him. His wife said, "It wasn't easy for him. So many times he would start to say something and stop right in the middle of a sentence. But today, I can honestly say, I haven't heard him make one nasty remark in six months. He's made a habit of saying something nice or not saying anything at all. I'm really proud of him."

When your negativity controls you, break your habit and do its opposite. Force yourself to leave your comfort zone and try something new. This concept is simple—but it may not be easy.

It's like the young man carrying a violin case heard on 57th Street in New York City. He asked an elderly gentleman, "Could you please tell me how to get to Carnegie Hall?" The elderly gentleman promptly replied, "Practice, practice, practice."

8. Relax and Reenergize

Finally, recognize that negative attitudes can be expensive. They can make you tense or lethargic, both of which are very costly. They can stop you from making decisions, setting up a plan of action, and going forward. They may cost you the success you want and need.

You may be the type who gets all tense when your attitude becomes too negative. That's understandable. If you constantly think gloom and doom are just around the corner, you're naturally going to get tense.

If this happens to you, try some deep-breathing exercises. As you inhale, think, "I breathe in peace." And as you exhale, think, "I breathe out tension." Let the tension flow out of your body.

If, on the other hand, your negative attitude tends to make you lethargic, then imagine yourself full of energy. See yourself achieving the goals you want to achieve. If you hold the image long enough, your negative attitude will start to dissipate.

Your Challenge

Tomorrow morning brings another day. I challenge you to rise and shine, and once and for all throw out the "rise and whine." Use these eight exercises to overcome your negativity and approach life with a positive attitude. You'll be glad you did, and so will everyone else in your world.

NEGATIVITY EXERCISES

Two Ways of Seeing Work Situations

Almost any situation can be seen positively or negatively. People with a positive attitude are skilled at "seeing" a situation differently, and they talk about it differently.

Listed in the following table are five examples. On the left you'll see the negative way a situation could be seen, and on the right you'll see the way a more positive person might see it.

Negative	Positive
1. It's never been done before.	I have the opportunity to be the first.
2. It's a waste of time.	I'll make sure I get something out of it.
3. I don't have the expertise.	I'll talk to those people who have the expertise.
4. There's not enough time.	I'll reorder my priorities to make time.
5. I'm not going to get through this interview.	I'm going to get good experience from this interview.

Take the following negative comments and rephrase them so they are more positive.

6. It's not my job.

7. It's a waste of my time applying for that job opening.

8. It's good enough.

9. There's no way it will work.

10. We don't have enough money in the budget to make all those changes.

11. We're understaffed.

12. My manager would never give me his/her support to do that.

13. It's too radical of a change.

14. I don't know much about that technology.

PART TWO

The Revolution

CHAPTER FOUR

Self-esteem

WHEN YOU LOVE YOURSELF
YOU DON'T HURT YOURSELF

The Pervasiveness of Low Self-esteem

After I delivered the keynote address at a national business convention, an audience member drew me aside. He said he had something to discuss with me.

"I've just been promoted to a very high position in my company," he said. "I'm scared to death. I've let them think that I know all about the job, that I'm extremely competent. But I don't think I can do it. I'll make a fool of myself!"

Have you ever felt that way? Have you ever been in a situation in which your self-esteem was somewhat shaky? Probably so. In a recent seminar, I asked the people in the audience to raise their hands if they had all the self-confidence they wanted and needed. Most people laughed. Only a few of them were able to raise their hands.

The strange thing is most people look confident and composed on the outside—but they've got too much self-doubt on the inside. Dr. Robert Schuller confirmed this in a national study. He claims most people don't have nearly enough self-esteem. They're like cars sputtering along on fuel that has too low an octane rating.

The Importance of Self-esteem

Thousands of years ago, Sirach wrote, "Don't underrate yourself. Humility deserves honor and respect, but a low opinion of yourself leads to sin."

In the twentieth century, Dr. Charles Mayo said, "I never knew a man to die of overwork, but I have known men to die of doubt." This self-esteem stuff isn't some fancy pop psychology trend or passing fad. Great authors throughout history from many cultures have known the value of self-esteem.

Recently, Dr. David McClelland completed twenty-five years of research trying to determine the number one factor in success. Much to his chagrin, he found out it wasn't his first idea, education; some people with doctoral degrees can't even get jobs washing dishes in a restaurant. In contrast, many people with nothing more than a high school education do very, very well.

Then McClelland thought the number one factor in success might be intelligence. But, of course, you know that's not the case either. Many brilliant people sit on their butts, going nowhere in life, while lots of folks with average intelligence go a long way.

After twenty-five years of research, McClelland concluded that the number one factor in success is self-esteem. High self-esteem is absolutely critical because your performance corresponds *exactly* to how you see yourself performing. Your view of yourself is the controlling mechanism in your life. If you cannot see yourself standing up in front of an audience and giving a speech without notes or nervousness, you will never be able to do it. If you cannot see yourself making cold calls without the fear of rejection, you will never be able to do it. And if you cannot see yourself being patient with your kids, you never will be. You perform exactly as you see yourself performing.

Dr. Maxwell Maltz, author of *Psycho-Cybernetics*, backs this up. He says your behavior is always consistent with your self-image. If you hold an image of yourself as a failure, you will fail, despite your best intentions to do otherwise. But if you see yourself as victorious, you will find some way to succeed, despite the presence of obstacles in your life.

The Self-esteem Choice

You need a powerful, positive sense of self-esteem. That's not even debatable. And the good news is that you can have it. Improving your self-esteem is simply a matter of choice and a bit of practice.

That's right, choice! Even though you may have some doubts, even though the balance sheet of your life may show more liabilities than assets, you can choose to believe in yourself. Sugar Ray Robinson, the boxing champ, knows that. He said, "To be a champ, you have to believe in yourself when nobody else will." And he chooses to do exactly that.

The same could be said for country singer Dolly Parton. She says, "I'm not offended by all the dumb blond jokes because I know that I'm not dumb . . . and I also know that I'm not blond." She chooses to believe in herself.

Senator Robert Taft, one of the great politicians of the twentieth century, lived out a similar self-esteem choice. Early in his political career, Taft went into hostile territory to make a speech. Someone threw an overripe tomato at him. It hit him in the chest and burst all over his face, glasses, and hair.

How did he respond? Did he react with anger? Lash out? Quit? No. He didn't even wipe his face, glasses, or hair. He just went on giving his speech and never even referred to the tomato. When he finished, he stepped down from the platform and said, "Good-bye, boys," in a friendly manner. As Senator Taft walked down the aisle toward the door, the once-hostile crowd gave him a standing ovation.

That's what I call class. Taft believed in himself, and so can you—if you choose to do so.

The Practice of Self-esteem

So how do you go about believing in yourself? You can build better, stronger self-esteem with practice using seven techniques. The process is not all that difficult. As master juggler Rob Peck says, "You don't have to believe in magic—because the real magic is in believing." The magic is in believing in yourself.

What's important about these seven techniques is they allow you to build a lasting self-esteem that never lets you down. And that's what you need. You don't need self-esteem that goes up and down, back and forth, depending on the circumstances. But that's the way a lot of people live. One day you make a sale, feel pretty good, and believe in yourself. The next day you lose a sale, feel rejected, and doubt yourself. Later on, you make a presentation at the staff meeting, get some negative feedback, and feel bad—until another project gets some praise. And so it goes, the self-esteem going up and down, back and forth. It's an awful way to live.

Of course, you may be wondering how all this self-esteem stuff relates to the overall theme of this book. The connection is quite simple. When your self-esteem is in great shape, you'll have a very positive attitude. And if you've got a very positive attitude, you'll have lots of self-esteem. When you build one, you build the other.

Some of the seven self-esteem practices are skills you use with other people, and some of them you have to do by yourself. In this chapter I'll focus on the four practices you do by yourself.

1. AFFIRM YOURSELF

Human beings have one major tool that other creatures do not have. We can determine, to some extent, how successful we're going to be by carefully choosing the words we tell ourselves.

In fact, rising above your own words is almost impossible. If you tell yourself that you just can't do something, you'll probably be right. And if you tell yourself you can do it, you'll also be right most of the time. This is called self-talk or affirmations. And successful people use positive affirmations on a regular basis. They affirm the kind of people they already are, or they affirm the kind of people they want to become.

A famous engineer, Charles Kettering, learned that the focus of your mind determines the results of your behavior, and he explained the process to his friend Joe.

Joe was skeptical, so Charles made a bet with him. He said he would buy a beautiful birdcage for his friend, who would hang it in the living room. He bet that Joe would have to put a bird in the cage. Joe took the bet, thinking it would be an easy bet to win.

Three months went by, during which time Joe had a large number of visitors. They all came into the living room, and of course, they immediately asked, "Where's the bird, Joe?"

Joe explained that he had never had a bird. But they didn't believe him. They said, "Joe, nobody has a beautiful birdcage like that without a bird in it!"

At night, Joe kept dreaming about their comments. Over and over he heard them say, "Nobody has a birdcage without a bird in it!" He kept thinking about it, until one day he found himself driving by a pet store. He peeked in the window. And as you can guess, when Charles came back to visit his friend, Joe had a beautiful bird in the beautiful birdcage.

A very similar thing happens when you affirm yourself. You are hanging empty birdcages in your mind. And you're not content until you fill the birdcages with belief and action.

I can't overemphasize this point. If you want to become a more positive person, you must spend a few minutes a day giving yourself positive affirmations. This is absolutely critical. You've got to get on the ball and talk to yourself positively.

Perhaps you remember the story of the golfer who found his ball on top of an anthill. He wondered what he was going to do, but then he decided to go for it. He took a huge swing, and whoosh, thousands of ants went flying, but the ball was still there. He took another huge swing, and thousands more ants went flying to their death. But the ball did not move. He was about to take one more swing when one of the remaining ants said to another, "If we don't get on the ball, we're going to die."

If you want higher self-esteem, you've got to get on the ball. You've got to tap into the power of positive affirmations. You've got to feed your mind if you want dramatically better results in your life and your career.

Of course, you may be wondering how to use affirmations. It can be as simple as affirming your lovability. Start with a simple sentence. Tell yourself, as many times as possible each day, "I like myself. I like myself. I like myself." Or say, "I love myself." Say it dozens of times throughout the day. It may be the most important thing you'll ever tell yourself—because eventually, your subconscious mind will accept your affirmation, and that, in turn, will build your self-esteem.

Of course it will feel a little silly. You'll wonder if you're really that good or if you're just kidding yourself. Your old self-doubts are bound to creep back in. They're used to having control of your mind and your attitude. But just ignore them and keep on affirming your lovability.

You need to affirm your *capability* as well. That's what the winners do. They affirm their capability rather than their "lose-ability."

It's like the little boy who walked onto the baseball field saying, "I'm the greatest hitter in the world." He threw up the ball, swung, missed, and said, "Strike one." He threw up the ball again, and once more he swung, missed, and said, "Strike two." He did that for three strikes in a row.

At that point he picked up his bat and ball. With a smile on his face, he walked off the field and said, "I'm the greatest pitcher in the world." He refused to use the language of a loser. He only talked about winning, and so should you.

To affirm your capability, you could affirm the fact that you have the knowledge and the ability to do what needs to be done. Remind yourself of past victories. Congratulate yourself on the good you have done and will do.

And as you do that, refuse to let any self-doubt enter your mind. Just tell yourself over and over, "I am filled with confidence, and I am competent." Eventually your subconscious mind will accept your affirmation, and you will become more capable.

Roger Bannister took this approach. Perhaps you remember that at one time it was considered impossible to run a mile in less than four minutes. People claimed the wind resistance would prevent it, and the runner's heart would beat so fast that the runner would drop dead. But in 1954, Roger Bannister ran the first sub-four-minute mile.

And how did he do it? He kept affirming his capability. He kept telling himself that he was the fastest and that he could run the mile in less than four minutes.

Winners know that words precede results. They know if they talk like losers, they'll end up losing. George Schultz, the former U.S. secretary of state, said, "The minute you start talking about what you're going to do if you lose, you have lost."

But the person who will not acknowledge defeat cannot be defeated. He's guaranteed to win in the long run.

After you've assured yourself of your capability, you need to affirm your ability to achieve. Bob Richards found out that winners affirm achievability all the time. As an Olympic pole-vaulter, and later as a TV spokesman for Wheaties, Richards took an extensive look at all the champions in all forms of athletic endeavor. He found that the vast majority of champions had somewhat "normal" bodies. They weren't born athletes, as some people like to think. But almost without exception the great athletes, the champions, did more than train their bodies. They also trained their minds using affirmations. They talked to themselves over and over again, affirming their ability to achieve and building their self-esteem.

You can use the same approach. First, think of a goal you want to achieve. It could be as simple as wanting to become more patient. Then select a key word like *patience* and speak the word fifty times in the morning and fifty times in the afternoon. Continue the practice for at least twenty-one days, and then when you're confronted with an irritating coworker or a bout of bad luck, you'll automatically respond with patience. You will have conditioned yourself to think and behave differently because you affirmed your goal's achievability.

I know this technique worked for me, and it will work for you. When nothing else seemed to heal the crippling illness I once had, I gave achievement affirmations a try. They worked, and I got healthy.

And affirmations have helped millions of other people achieve their goals. I hear it all the time. My clients tell me how they moved from the bottom to the top in their industry or how they easily lost fifty pounds when they got into the habit of using affirmations.

So if you're not affirming achievability, you're losing out. You're not achieving everything you could achieve.

George Haines, the great swimming coach from Santa Clara, California, knew that secret. That's why he could say—honestly—that his team had won dozens of world-record plaques. And that's why, at one time, his team was breaking records so fast they literally couldn't make the plaques fast enough.

Of course, outsiders may have thought that Coach Haines was merely lucky. They may have thought that he was a better recruiter or that he had better athletes on his team. Not at all. He simply took the local kids from the neighborhood and turned them into world champs by changing their self-esteem.

As soon as his swimmers came out of the locker room and splashed into the pool, Haines would run up and down the side of the pool shouting, "Come on, baby! You can do it! You're a great one! Three seconds faster! I believe in you! You are a winner!" He was constantly affirming their achievability because he knew that would build their self-esteem and lead to triumph after triumph.

At the end of every tournament, the kids would come out of the pool with tears streaming down their cheeks. They would hug their coach and thank him for the gift of self-esteem he had implanted in them. But, of course, the real secret was that he got the kids to talk to themselves that same way all day long. They would affirm the achievability of winning, saying over and over, "I'm the fastest. I'm a champion. I'm a winner."

These affirmations are even backed up scientifically. In fact, a great deal of research shows they really work. Dr. Maxwell Maltz wrote about that in *Psycho-Cybernetic Principles for Creative Living*. He wrote about a twenty-day test where two groups of students worked to increase their effectiveness as basketball sharpshooters. One group practiced shooting at the basket every day; their marksmanship improved 24 percent by the twentieth day. The other group devoted twenty minutes a day to affirming they were throwing the ball into the basket. Incredibly, their accuracy soared 23 percent. Affirmations take the guesswork out of your future success.

I encourage you to give affirmations a good try. Talk to yourself positively. Let your positive affirmations sweep away the old, negative influences in your life. And let them build your self-esteem as they strengthen your positive attitude.

2. SURVEY YOUR STRENGTHS

You can also build your self-esteem through your awareness. Are you aware of all your strengths, talents, gifts, and blessings? You've got a bunch of them, that's for sure. The question is, do you know what they are? The greater your awareness of your strengths, the stronger your self-esteem will be.

Unfortunately, lots of people fail to see their strengths. They act like some of the frustrated, ignorant creatures in the animal kingdom. If you put a buzzard in a pen six or eight feet square, for example, with the top entirely open, the bird will remain a prisoner despite his ability to fly. The buzzard is used to starting his flight with a ten- to twelve-foot run. Without the space to run, he won't even attempt to fly. He'll remain a prisoner for life in a jail that has no top.

Likewise, if you drop a bumblebee into an open tumbler he will stay there until he dies. He keeps on looking for some way out through the bottom of the glass. He never sees his means of escape out through the top. You may be like these animals. You may not see all the strengths you have. So I recommend a two-step process.

First, survey your strengths. Get out a paper and pencil. I want you to complete exercise 2, the Thirty-Day Self-esteem Builder, at the end of this chapter. Write out your answers and review them every day for thirty days. I know you'll have more self-esteem and a stronger, more positive attitude at the end of the month, because I've seen this exercise work miracles in the lives of hundreds of thousands of people.

The exercise comes out of my work with college students years ago. I would see way too many students spend four years in college, preparing for a job, and then blow it all away during a job interview. Oh, sure, those students might have had good grades, decent recommendations, and some appropriate work experience, but if they didn't project a self-confident image during the interview, they typically didn't get the job.

Then it dawned on me. The job interviewer couldn't be expected to know what the student had going for himself if the student didn't even know those things. So I told my students to write down two hundred things they do well before they went to a job interview. Perhaps they were honest, hardworking, persevering, and well educated. Maybe they got along well with others, respected authority, and were upbeat and positive.

Even though the students never showed their lists to the interviewers, the lists gave them greater confidence. They knew they were going into the interview with something to *give*, not just get from a prospective employer. And the results were dramatically better.

I advise you to do likewise. Survey your strengths. Write them all down. It will give you a much stronger sense of self-esteem.

The next step in knowing your strengths is to use your strengths. You are responsible for using your own strengths. There is simply no acceptable excuse for doing anything else. You can get off your assets and do something anytime you want.

That's what one marathon runner did. By the time he was fifty years old, he had run fifty marathons. That's amazing enough, fifty marathons, each 26 miles, 365 yards in length. But this man had no feet, no legs, just stumps. A reporter asked him, "How do you do it?" He simply said, "You don't lean backwards." What great advice! You don't lean backwards in life. You use your assets, and you move forward.

One lady figured that out. She lost her husband at about the same time they had planned to retire and travel together. They had made all their plans and were looking forward to the fulfillment of their lifelong dream. But a month after he retired, her husband suddenly died.

All of life seemed to come to an end for his wife. She put a tombstone on her husband's grave that said, "The light of my life has gone out." I'm sure you can understand.

But with the passage of time and the use of her strengths, she decided to keep busy, meet people, and keep on living. Two years later she met another wonderful man and began to build a new life.

When it was time to get married, she told her pastor, "I'm going to have to change that line on the tombstone. I can't say 'the light of my life has gone out.'"

Her wise pastor said, "No. I think all you have to do is add another line: 'I struck a new match!'"

Of course using their strengths is easier for some people than for others. Some people encounter more obstacles than others. That's life. But as Naomi Judd so aptly said, "You're only a victim once. The next time you're an accomplice."

You may argue with me and say you're stuck in a relationship or stuck in a job, and that you have no choice. You may truly believe you are the victim of circumstances and that you have no ability to change anything. But that's simply not true. You almost always have choices.

Although you may not like some of your choices, you still have choices. And as soon as you realize you made the choice to be where you're at, you'll have less stress and more self-esteem. You'll know you've got some control over your life, and that you can change it if you wish.

Let's say, for example, that you and I are having a conversation. You tell me that you hate your job, so I tell you to quit. You might say, "I can't. I have to stay here. I have no choice."

But you do have a choice. The alternative to the job you hate may be a worse job. The alternative may be going on welfare, or letting your parents pay your bills. Or the alternative may be letting your kids and family starve.

The fact is that you do have choices. And you made a choice. You examined the options, and the one you chose was better than the alternatives. When you understand that, you realize you're in control, and you can't help but have a better attitude about the situation.

Are you aware of your strengths? Are you using them? A woman named Karen taught me to do that on a very personal level many years ago. She was sitting right in front of me, in the middle of my audience, for an all-day program on self-esteem. And even though she was confined to a wheelchair, I couldn't help but notice her great smile, attractive appearance, and obvious confidence.

She wheeled up to me at the end of the workshop and said, "You know, you are right. All day long people talk about their problems and difficulties. Don't they realize what they have? They have legs that work. I'd give just about anything to have legs that work."

Then she related her story. She was born healthy, but at age two she developed spinal cancer, a disease that forever after made it impossible for her to walk. But she said, "The strangest thing is watching home movies of me before the cancer came. My father has movies of me playing with our puppy or searching for Easter eggs. It's weird to see myself running and walking when I have no recollection of ever moving. I'd love to have what everyone else takes for granted: legs that work."

Karen went on to say the lack of mobility didn't stop her. She made a list of what she could do, made sure she used her strengths, and had a very successful career as a counselor and later as a manager.

3. TAKE RISKS

Some two thousand years ago, Socrates said, "Fortune is not on the side of the fainthearted." His words are still true today. You can't expect to win any races without courage and a strong belief in yourself.

In more recent research, Dr. Bruce Larson confirmed that. After interviewing dozens of experts in the fields of psychology and human potential, Larson discovered one thing on which they all agreed. They all said that if you want high self-esteem, you've got to take some risks. You can't live in a comfort zone, be afraid of change, and feel good about yourself.

What about you? Are you a risk taker? Are you the kind of person who truly believes in yourself and tends to go for your goals? Eula Weaver certainly was.

At age seventy-seven, Eula was paralyzed with a stroke. It would have been easy for her to think, "This is it. I'm at the age most people die, so I must be on my way out."

Not Eula. She could hardly walk, but the doctors gave her two choices: (1) spend the rest of her life as an invalid, allow herself to be hand-fed, and get ready to die, or (2) get out of bed and start walking no matter how much it hurt.

Eula decided to go for it, to take a risk. Some time later, the newspaper featured Eula in her jogging suit running a mile a day at age eighty-eight.

Are you a believer like Eula, or are you the kind of person who doubts yourself and tends to hold back? Do you live too much of your life in a comfort zone? Do you go to staff meetings and sit in the same place by the same people? Do you say what people want to hear in the staff meeting but say something else after the meeting? Are you in the same job, doing the same things, year after year? Are you afraid of trying new processes or going for the job you really want?

And what about your personal life? Are you reluctant to take risks? Do you stuff your feelings rather than share them? Do you have a hard time speaking in public, talking to strangers, or trying something different? Do you sit in the same church pew week after week because sitting next to people you already know is comfortable?

People with low self-esteem—and a negative attitude—tend to live in a comfort zone. They're terribly afraid of change because they don't have the confidence to handle it. So they justify and rationalize the status quo, giving a million reasons why change isn't necessary or why it won't work. They stay stuck in the mud, rigidly adhering to their particular points of view or their ways of doing things, like the man who was told by the fortune teller, "You'll be poor, unhappy, and miserable until you're fifty."

"Then what?" asked the man.

"By that time," the fortune teller said, "you'll be used to it."

People with low self-esteem get used to it. But people with high self-esteem—or those who want to have higher self-esteem—see it quite differently. They know they've got to go for it once in a while. They know they've got to take some risks if they want to feel better about themselves and win some of the bigger prizes in life.

They take the advice of Sir Edmund Hillary, who was the first man to successfully reach the summit of Mt. Everest. He said, "Aim high! There is little virtue in easy victory."

Hillary wasn't advocating foolish living; he was advocating bold living. He said you need to do your homework and study each problem or opportunity that comes your way. Learn as much as you can about each of them, make a decision, and then take bold action. Don't give in to faintheartedness. Faintheartedness always gets faint results.

Babe Ruth knew that. One of the things that made him a great baseball player was the fact that he would swing at any pitch that was any good at all. Sure, he struck out a lot, but he also hit more home runs than any other player of his time.

If you start taking a few more risks—intelligent risks—I can assure you that you'll feel better about yourself. You will build your self-esteem, and you will build a stronger, more positive attitude in all parts of your life.

I learned that lesson when I was twenty years old. I came down with such a serious case of rheumatoid arthritis that I could barely get around. My knees were swollen, my legs wouldn't straighten, and my neck barely moved. I even had difficulty eating solid foods. My whole body was affected.

I was back under the care of my mother. She would put pillows under my knees at night to relieve the pressure. And she would drive me back and forth to my classes at the university because I could no longer drive. Talk about a blow to my self-esteem.

I went to several doctors, and they all said there was no cure for arthritis, especially rheumatoid arthritis. They even predicted that I would end up in a wheelchair. My self-esteem hit the skids. I wanted to be out running, going to dances, and doing all the other fun things to do at college, but I couldn't.

Out of desperation, I went to a chiropractor. The man I found was rather helpful but also a weird character. He weighed 350 pounds, had seven teeth, and had horrible body odor. He used his great big hands to jerk my head around, push on my back, and massage my legs.

But the strange thing was he would ask me the same questions week after week. He'd ask, "Are you dating? Do you have a girlfriend?" And I'd always say no, because in my mind that was too risky. I didn't look cool and couldn't get around very well. I thought I had enough problems without risking rejection.

So I stayed in my comfort zone. I didn't date. I just felt sorry for myself.

After six months of asking me the same questions, the chiropractor got a little angry at me. He told me to get out there, to ask someone for a date, and have some fun. He said, "So what if they turn you down? They'll all be dead in a hundred years and won't remember anyway!"

It finally made sense to me. I realized that if I didn't take the risk of asking somebody out, I would put myself down for being too chicken to even ask. If I took the risk and the girl said yes, I would feel pretty good. And even if she said no, I could respect myself for having had the courage to try.

You always gain by taking risks. You either realize you can do it, or you gain respect for yourself for trying, which is a great boost to your self-esteem as well your overall attitude.

Of course, leaving your comfort zone and taking risks is scary. I know that. But I also know that you stand to gain in two significant ways if you take more risks.

First, you're likely to have better relationships. In fact, Dr. Bruce Larson found a clear connection between people who take risks with openness and people who have stronger, healthier relationships.

Unfortunately, millions of people, even married people, have never in their whole lifetimes experienced good, healthy, juicy intimacy. Somewhere along the way they got hurt in a relationship. The other person spoke an unkind word, used a sarcastic tone of voice, or forgot a promise that was made.

When they got hurt, they told themselves that they had been hurt enough and they could no longer trust their spouse or anyone else. Then they built walls to keep out the hurt. They pulled back and stopped taking any communication risks that would let the other people in their relationships get close to them. But the walls also kept out the intimacy, and the relationship soured.

As poet John Barrymore wrote, "We are as sick as we are secret." In other words, if you don't tear the walls down, if you refuse to be gutsy, open, honest, and vulnerable, you'll never have a healthy relationship. And you won't feel good about yourself as a part of that relationship.

The second benefit of taking more risks—intelligent risks—is that you'll probably live longer. This was another of Dr. Larson's discoveries. Folks who keep trying new things feel better about themselves and live longer.

And yet I hear so many people who are mistaken on this point. They think they can retire at age sixty-five, sit back, take it easy, and do nothing. They don't realize that people who take that approach die sooner.

When I first came across Larson's research, I was surprised, to say the least. So I asked my corporate clients about this retire-and-die phenomenon. Did they ever see this? And their answer was a resounding yes. Honeywell told me that 50 percent of their engineers were dead within two years of retirement. IBM-Vermont said half of their employees were dead within eighteen months of retirement. And the United Auto Workers reported that their typical retiree received seventeen Social Security checks before he or she passed away.

The common denominator in these early deaths seems to be a lack of risk taking after retirement. These retirees were the kinds of folks who focused all their energies on their jobs. Indeed, their jobs had meant everything to them. Their jobs had been the sources of their self-esteem. But now the jobs were gone. So they sat back and vegetated because they didn't know much about taking on new and different challenges.

Quite simply, you can't feel good about yourself, living your whole life in a comfort zone. And you may not live as long if you're not taking a few risks. So go for it once in a while. Step outside your comfort zone. Take a risk.

4. GRANT YOURSELF GENTLENESS

The first three self-esteem skills can be and should be used any-time. But what do you do when the tough times come? Does your self-esteem get fired up or burnt up? Do you put yourself down, or are you able to maintain your self-confidence? And does your attitude stay as positive as you would like it to be?

You can maintain your self-esteem and positive attitude in tough times if you use this fourth skill. If you grant yourself gentleness, if you forgive yourself, if you are gracious with yourself, you'll be okay. I recommend the following process.

First, *laugh at yourself.* That doesn't mean that you tear into yourself or tear yourself apart. And it doesn't mean that you pre-tend something is good when it isn't. You simply look for what is funny in your situation. As someone once said, "Accept the fact that some days you're the pigeon, and some days you're the statue."

You may bemoan the fact you're getting older and losing some of your youthful energy. Learn to laugh at yourself. My grandfather said, "I'm always glad to have birthdays. It's not having a birthday that doesn't excite me."

People who can laugh at themselves are the ones who have the most joy. The comedian George Burns illustrated that by the way he lived and the way he talked.

When George was asked what it was like to get old, he gave a wonderful answer. He said, "You know you're getting old when you stoop down to tie your shoelaces and wonder what else you could do while you're down there." He was able to laugh at himself.

Can you be as gracious with yourself? Are you able to find the humor in your situation? I know it will preserve your self-esteem during the tough times.

Maybe you're being teased or criticized. Maybe it hurts. Sometimes the best response is a light-hearted—not mean-spirited—little joke.

Justice Oliver Wendell Holmes once attended a meeting in which he was the shortest man present. "Dr. Holmes," quipped a friend, "I should think you'd feel rather small among us big fellows."

"I do," replied Holmes. "I feel like a dime among pennies."

The next step in the process is to *focus on the "how" questions.* When you screw up, when you experience a major setback, you will either get better—or bitter. No other alternatives exist. That's just the way it is.

The people who get bitter ask themselves *why* questions. They respond to their disappointments by asking why they have to go through this or that. They spend hours and sometimes weeks, months, and years trying to figure out why. Why do I always have to be the one to clean up? Why didn't I get that new position at corporate headquarters? Why didn't God heal me?

When you keep asking yourself why you have to go through something, you're basically telling yourself that life has treated you unfairly. Those thoughts, repeated often enough, will make you bitter.

The truth is, you'll have a lot of *why* questions in life for which you'll never have an answer. That doesn't mean you shouldn't look for answers. You should. Finding answers is what education is all about. Just don't get stuck on *why*.

By contrast, people who get better ask a different question. When disappointments come, they ask themselves *how* they can *grow* through the situation. In other words, they consciously look for the lessons in the loss. They know they can learn something in the midst of disappointment, and they're going to find it.

The underlying lesson may be professional; for instance, the loss of a job promotion can tell you it's time to update your skills. Or the lesson may be personal, such as a sense of burnout teaching you to say no to some things in life. Whatever the case, every loss has a lesson.

In fact, you can learn a lot more from the bad times than the good times. The bad times make you look for new and better ways to achieve your goals. They push you to make the changes you need to make, and build your character—if you focus on how you can grow through the disappointment.

A verse in the Bible says you should give thanks in all things. That may sound strange or even impossible to do in the midst of difficulty, but the advice is great. If you look for the lesson in the difficulty, you can give thanks, and you will become a better person. After all, fruit grows in the valleys of difficulty, not on the mountaintops of success.

Finally, to preserve your self-esteem in times of difficulty, you must *take responsibility*. I know that's a very unpopular position to take. Our culture has shifted dramatically in the last fifty years. It used to be that most people lived by the philosophy, *If it is to be, it's up to me.* In other words, you are responsible for your life. Good or bad, you have to make the best out of the life you have.

Now, however, a large number of people in our culture refuse to take responsibility. They want to blame someone else for their misfortunes. So you see the craziest lawsuits—where one person blames the maker of Hostess Twinkies for turning him into a murderer and someone else blames a manufacturer for producing a product that makes him sick, even though he freely chooses to consume too much of the product.

I once saw a sign that read, "Frustration is not having anybody to blame but yourself."

What about you? When things go wrong, do you look for other people to blame? Or do you take responsibility for making things better? The first response will keep you stuck. The second response will preserve your self-esteem.

Concluding Thoughts

Too many people crawl through their lives and their careers, defeated and afraid. They don't even come close to using all their potential or having all the joy they might want. Of course, some may try to cover that up by appearing pulled together, but beneath it all they are frightened people with poor self-esteem.

Well, it doesn't have to be that way. I just gave you four ways to improve your self-esteem. They all work if you apply them, and I encourage you to do so. Pick out a few techniques and master them. Do the exercises at the end of this chapter. And you'll find that the stronger your self-esteem becomes, the better your attitude will be.

That's why I keep a little card in my desk just to remind myself to keep working on my self-esteem. It reads:

If there is self-esteem in the soul, there will be happiness in the person.

If there is happiness in the person, there will be harmony in the home.

If there is harmony in the home, there will be order in the nation.

If there is order in the nation, there will be peace in the world.

SELF-ESTEEM EXERCISES

1. Affirm Your Belief in Yourself

a. Choose to believe in yourself a little bit more than you did last week.

b. Tell yourself over and over, "I like myself. I believe in myself."

c. Say it every day, several times a day, for at least twenty-one days. You will notice a strengthening in your self-esteem.

2. Thirty-Day Self-esteem Builder

a. Character assets: List ten character assets you have—such things as honesty, reliability, a sense of humor, or any positive personality traits that come to mind.

b. Skills and abilities: Take out a sheet of paper and write down twenty things you're good at. You may include your natural talents or the education and training you've received. You may want to list skills that you use on the job, at home, or as a hobby. If you can't think of twenty, ask your friends and coworkers to point out a few.

c. Physical assets: List ten physical assets you possess—such things as an attractive smile, a good head of hair, or a fairly healthy body. Just remember, you are listing *assets*, not signs of perfection. No one thinks his or her body is as good as it could be.

d. Relationship assets: Think of people who love you and believe in you. They could be people from your personal or professional life, and they could be alive or dead. They may be people you see often or seldom see. List ten people who care about you and whom you can depend on.

e. Blessings: Take out another sheet of paper and list one hundred blessings in your life. List things for which you are thankful. Maybe you have a job, a spouse, some kids, a place to live, or a little extra money. They're all blessings. Write down one hundred of your blessings.

f. Personal changes: Write down five things you want to change in your personal life. Focus on changes you want to see in yourself, not changes you want to see in other people. For example, you may want more self-confidence, more assertiveness, or more skill at meeting new people.

g. Professional changes: Write down five things you want to change in your professional life. You may want, for example, more education, a position of greater responsibility, or a whole new career.

h. Morning self-esteem builder:

(1) Before getting dressed, stand in front of the mirror and affirm some of your character assets. Then say to yourself five times, "I love you."

(2) While dressing, think about the people who love you and the things you are grateful for.

(3) Pick one thing from your list of things to change about yourself. Let that be part of your focus today. Do something, anything, to make a little progress in this area of your life.

i. Evening self-esteem reinforcement:

(1) Write down all the positive things you did today and the good feelings you had.

(2) Write down which your most outstanding character assets of the day were and why they were outstanding.

(3) Record your successes, no matter how small, on your chosen change item for the day. Remember, it's progress you're after, not perfection.

CHAPTER FIVE

Relationships

HANG AROUND PEOPLE WHO LIFT YOU UP, NOT THOSE WHO BRING YOU DOWN

You can strengthen your self-esteem all by yourself. You really can. But the truth is that you don't live in a vacuum. You live and work with other people, and they can make building your self-esteem and maintaining your positive attitude a great deal more difficult or a great deal easier.

That's why you need to choose your relationships very carefully. And that's also why you need to know how to receive the best from people, as well as how to deflect the worst. This chapter will look at the three main people skills you must develop to build and maintain strong self-esteem.

1. Listen to Praise

If you ever doubt yourself, if you ever struggle with low self-esteem, it may be due to the fact that you've received lots of negatives from other people. You may have gotten too many negative comments from your family members when you were growing up, or perhaps you got too much negative feedback from your teachers, bosses, or coworkers over the years. And today, as you may well know, the number one job complaint is that you can do a hundred things right and not hear a darn thing about it, but do one thing wrong and your superiors are all over you.

But it just stands to reason that if your low self-esteem was caused by other people's negatives, then other people's positives can help build your self-esteem, if you *listen* to their positives.

Unfortunately, many people don't listen. They reject the compliments of others. When they're told their work is good, many people say that it was nothing, that anyone could have done it, that there's no need to mention it. When you compliment their outfit, they comment on how old it is or that they got it on sale.

In fact, you may have seen people go back and forth, giving and rejecting compliments. One person says how much he likes the outfit while the other one says it's not so great. The first person rewords the compliment and the second person rejects it again. After a while, the first person starts to think the outfit isn't so nice and stops the flow of compliments.

Do you refuse to accept the compliments of others? Do you shove them back in their faces? If you do, then chances are you've trained people not to praise you. You've trained them to figure, *Fine, to heck with it.* And chances are you end up with lower self-esteem, a negative attitude, and the feeling of being taken for granted. You end up wondering why no one ever seems to notice the work you do.

A woman who attended one of my workshops was able to relate this scenario to her life. She said, "I'm a full-time nurse; my husband is a full-time businessman. On Saturdays I bake bread. My husband loves my homemade bread."

Now, if you've ever made bread you know that it takes a lot of work. You have to mix up the ingredients and let the dough rise. Then you push it back down, and let it rise again. This woman said, "I was getting ticked off. I was spending all day Saturday making bread for my husband while he sat in the family room guzzling a six-pack of beer. Then one day I turned to him and said, 'Hey, buddy. I work as hard as you do all week long. I've been making this bread for you, not for me. I could not care less about this stuff. And you don't even bother to thank me.'"

Her husband replied, "Just a minute, honey. You know that your bread is my favorite food. I've told you a hundred times, maybe a thousand times how much I like that bread. And every time I said that I liked it, you said, 'Oh, no, no. It's too heavy, too dark, too light, too crusty, or too spongy.'" She said at that moment she realized she had trained him to stop giving her compliments, and now she was blaming him for it.

The simple way to get the compliments you need and deserve is to acknowledge every one you get. Respond with a simple, gracious, genuine, heartfelt "Thanks." Your acknowledgment feeds your self-esteem, builds your positive attitude, and shows respect for the other person's opinion. It's a total win-win situation.

2. Inject Your Individuality

Now that's a strange phrase. You're probably wondering what it means to inject your individuality. It means two things: (1) being yourself, and (2) standing up for yourself. Neither of these things is easy, but either of them will build your self-esteem as well as your overall attitude.

Of course, it's difficult to "be yourself." There's a lot of pressure in school and business to act a certain way or be like certain people.

That's what one twelfth grader in Regina, Saskatchewan, wrote about when he was asked to turn in a poem for his English class. It was simply entitled, "About School."

> He always wanted to say things. But no one understood.
>
> He always wanted to explain things. But no one cared.
>
> So he drew.
>
> Sometimes he would just draw and it wasn't anything. He wanted to carve it in stone or write it in the sky.
>
> He would lie out on the grass and look up in the sky and it would be only him and the sky and the things inside him that needed saying.
>
> And it was after that that he drew the picture. It was a beautiful picture. He kept it under the pillow and let no one see it.
>
> And he would look at it every night and think about it. And when it was dark and his eyes were closed, he could still see it.
>
> And it was all of him. And he loved it.
>
> When he started school he brought it with him. Not to show anyone, but just to have it with him like a friend.
>
> It was funny about school.
>
> He sat in a square, brown desk like all the other square, brown desks and he thought it should be red.
>
> And his room was a square, brown room. Like all the other rooms. And it was tight and close. And stiff.

He hated to hold the pencil and the chalk, with his arm stiff and his feet flat on the floor, stiff, with his teacher watching and watching.

And then he had to write numbers. And they weren't anything. They were worse than the letters that could be something if you put them together.

And the numbers were tight and square and he hated the whole thing.

The teacher came and spoke to him. She told him to wear a tie like all the other boys. He said he didn't like them and she said it didn't matter.

After that they drew. And he drew all yellow and it was the way he felt about morning. And it was beautiful.

The teacher came and smiled at him. "What's this?" she said. "Why don't you draw something like Ken's drawing? Isn't that beautiful?"

It was all questions.

After that his mother bought him a tie and he always drew airplanes and rocket ships like everyone else.

And he threw the old picture away.

And when he would lay out alone looking at the sky, it was big and blue and all of everything, but he wasn't anymore.

He was square inside and brown, and his hands were stiff, and he was like anyone else. And the thing inside him that needed saying didn't need saying anymore.

It had stopped pushing. It was crushed. Stiff. Like everything else.

I don't know much about that young fellow. He just turned in his assignment and committed suicide two weeks later.

Yes, being yourself can be mighty tough. That's why some people wear masks, especially those with low self-esteem. They cover up their real selves because they don't think anyone would like them the way they really are. They try to figure out what kind of person others would like and pretend to be that kind of person.

Of course, this strategy is dangerous. If you fool people, if you're able to wear a convincing mask, you're in trouble when you get complimented. The compliments make you doubt your true self. You know that people like your mask, but you're not sure if they like you.

What about you? Do you wear any masks? Or are you able to be yourself? This ability is a prerequisite for high self-esteem.

When I speak in the business world, I'm often amused by the number of people who wear masks of self-importance. They pretend to be more important than they really are. They come across as know-it-alls, acting arrogant or superior, too busy to be bothered by others. They appear to have too much self-esteem, when, in fact, just the opposite is the case.

I remember one confident young man who broke through someone else's mask. He had tried over and over again to get an appointment with a certain executive, but with no success.

Finally, he was able to see the man's secretary. He gave her an envelope with his card and a note inside. She delivered it, and the executive came right out.

Of course she wondered how the young man had done it. Simple. He had written, "This morning I talked to God for fifteen minutes. How come I can't talk to you?"

He got the results he wanted by being assertive, and he probably felt pretty good about it. If you want more self-esteem and a more positive attitude, you've got to be yourself, and you've got to stand up for yourself.

Are you able to do that? Are you able to put up boundaries? Are you able to ask for what you need? Are you able to say no?

People with low self-esteem have difficulty doing such things. They think standing up for themselves is rude or selfish. It's not "nice."

Of course, there's nothing wrong with being nice, but some people take it too far. They think if they just go along with others and behave submissively, others will like them. And "nice guys" need other people to like them because they don't like themselves all that much.

Lou Holtz, the legendary football coach, put it very well when he said, "If you are a parent and it is desperately important that your kids like you, you will never have their respect." In other words, it takes a lot of guts and a good dose of self-esteem to stand up for yourself, say no, and lay down the rules—even with your own kids.

To maintain your own self-esteem, you've got to stand up for yourself. You can't let others take advantage of you and still feel good about yourself.

So what do you do when you feel cheated or disrespected? Do you speak out assertively and appropriately, or do you just let it go? When you go to a fancy restaurant for a special occasion and order an expensive steak and get a burnt sacrifice instead, what do you do? Are you able to say that the steak is unacceptable? Do you ask for a different steak? Or do you simply let it go, deciding never to enter that restaurant again?

Your self-esteem goes up when you stand up for yourself. And your self-esteem goes down when you fail to do so.

I attended a seminar by Father John Powell, author of *The Secret of Staying in Love*. And I remember the example he gave of what happened in a relationship when someone refused to stand up for herself. It revolved around a woman who was a good mother, wife, and professional. She was attractive and seemed to have herself together in so many ways.

In spite of that, she had a husband who cheated on her with several girlfriends. He eventually dropped her to take off with another woman, and she, of course, was angry and heartbroken. So she came to Father Powell for counseling. She wanted to get her life back together, and she wanted to make sure she never again ended up in a similar situation.

One counseling session was particularly helpful. She talked about the way she waited at the door to hug and kiss her husband when he came home from work each day. It puzzled Father Powell, so he asked her, "What were you saying to yourself, inside your head, when you were hugging and kissing him?" She said, "Oh, I guess I was saying 'Please, please love me. Let me know I'm okay.'"

And why was she thinking that? Why did she need her husband's approval so desperately? Because he was so very critical of her. If the house was immaculate, dinner was wonderful, and the kids were well behaved, he might give her a hug or kiss. But if things didn't meet his approval, he would not talk to her all night.

She said, "I worried all day long about whether dinner would meet his approval, if things would be good enough. I thought if I hugged and kissed him at the door, maybe I could soften him up a bit."

On the surface, it looked like she was giving love, but in reality she was begging for love. And nobody can love or respect a beggar forever. She needed to stand up for herself. She needed to stop playing the nice guy and say, "I'm your wife, and I have a right to your fidelity. Yes, it's nice to have a clean house and a great meal all the time, but it's not always possible. And I don't want your love to be conditional on those things."

He might have left her anyway. But if she had stood up for herself, she could have at the very least kept her own self-respect.

By contrast, a person with high self-esteem is much more assertive. He stands up for himself, like the man with a pretzel stand in front of a large Chicago office building.

One day a businessman came out of the building, plunked down a quarter, and went on without taking a pretzel. The same routine went on every day for three weeks. Finally, the man running the stand spoke up and said, "Sir, excuse me. May I have a word with you?"

The businessman said, "I know what you're going to say. You're going to ask me why I give you a quarter every day and don't take a pretzel."

The pretzel man said, "Not at all. I just want to tell you that the price is now thirty-five cents."

That's standing up for yourself. Do a bit more of that, and you'll see an immediate improvement in your self-esteem and overall attitude.

3. Nurture Connectedness

You were not designed to be alone, and you're not equipped for loneliness. In fact, both will kill off your self-esteem and sour your attitude.

According to Dr. James Lynch, a medical researcher at Johns Hopkins University, loneliness is the number one physical killer in America. In his book, *The Broken Heart*, he provides a decade of research results to back this claim. He found that those who live alone have premature death rates anywhere from two to ten times higher than individuals who live with others.

In essence, you've got to hang around some people. But not just anybody. You should surround yourself with the right kind of people. As Mom said, "Choose your friends wisely."

The people around you always rub off on you. Perhaps you've noticed that kids with bad grades hang around other kids with bad grades. And people with marriage problems often have friends with marriage problems.

The people you choose to be with can make a huge difference in your self-esteem and attitude. And only two kinds of people exist: those who lift you up and those who pull you down.

So you've got to choose your relationships, your business associates, and even your acquaintances very carefully. You've got to be extremely cautious about spending too much time with negative people or the losers in life. If you don't release these kinds of people, or keep your distance, you'll end up resembling them.

Also, choose your coaches and counselors wisely. You can't just go to anyone for help or listen to anyone for advice, because who you pick may determine how well you do. Lou Holtz made this very clear to me. Lou said to me once, "If you go to people who never did anything or accomplished anything, they will tell you you can't do it. But if you go to those who have accomplished a lot, they'll give you encouragement."

So how do you choose the right kinds of people? And what kinds of connections will raise your self-esteem and boost your attitude? I've found several things that work.

First, *go where you are celebrated instead of where you are tolerated.* Don't spend time in those places that don't celebrate you, and don't waste your life on people who do not value you. Move on.

Some people are out to get you. And other people just put up with you. Avoid them if at all possible. They make it very difficult for you to believe in yourself.

For instance, think of the story of the captain of a sinking ship. The captain turned to his three remaining sailors and said, "Men, this business about a captain going down with his ship is nonsense. There's a three-man life raft on board, and I'm going to be on it. To see who will come with me, I will ask you each one question. The one who can't answer the question will stay behind."

He turned to one sailor and said, "Here's the first question. What unsinkable ship went down when it hit an iceberg?" The first sailor answered, "The *Titanic*, sir." "Good," said the captain.

"On to the second question," the captain turned to another sailor. "How many people perished?" The second sailor said, "One thousand five hundred and seventeen, sir." "Right," said the captain.

"Now for the third question," as the captain turned to the third sailor, "What were their names?"

So go where you are celebrated instead of tolerated.

Then, remember to *spend time with believers*. Spend time with people who believe in you, because they make it easier for you to believe in yourself.

I'm amazed at how many people will spend time with just about anyone. They'll spend their lunchtime with coworkers who do nothing but gripe about the company and the customers. And they'll spend their free time with "friends" who do nothing but pick them apart. No wonder these people have a hard time maintaining their self-esteem or staying positive.

A person does not automatically qualify as a friend just because you work or live around him, or because you've known her a long time. Proximity and longevity don't necessarily make someone good for you. As Henry Ford put it, "Who is your best friend? Your best friend is he or she who helps you bring out of yourself the best that is in you."

I can't overstress how important it is to spend time with those who believe in you. Avoid the negative folks if at all possible and whenever appropriate. Even if the negative people don't say anything, your subconscious mind will always pick up their beliefs about you, and their beliefs will always hurt your self-esteem and your performance.

Psychologists proved that a long time ago when they studied the "self-fulfilling prophecy." In one experiment twelve students were given plain, ordinary rats. Six of the students were told they had highly intelligent rats. The other six were told that they had the dumbest, laziest, slowest rats that could be found.

Both groups were told to teach their rats to run through a maze. At the end of the six months, the first group of students had developed the most amazing, high-performing rats you could imagine. They could go through any maze with ease. The other group had failed to teach their rats even the most basic maneuver.

In both cases, the rats were genetically the same, but the beliefs of the students were different. Those who expected achievement got achievement, and those who anticipated failure got failure. So spend your time with people who believe in you.

Third, *stay in contact with encouragers*, or sideliners, as they're called in the Special Olympics. Each athlete has someone on the sidelines who showers him with praise and encouragement. And as a result, the athlete is able to overcome feelings of inadequacy and discover his full potential.

Do you have one or more sideliners in your life? I hope so. As I study successful people, I find that very few of them are self-made successes. Almost every truly successful person has a sideliner in his life.

If you've got a sideliner, that's great. If you need one, get one. And if you're wondering what to look for—or whether or not your present associations qualify as sideliners—let me suggest these guidelines.

Sideliners comfort you. They see that you're hurt when others don't notice. And they offer solid proof of your worth. When you doubt yourself, they remind you how good you really are. As a professional speaker, I am occasionally discouraged by attendees who don't care or won't try anything I teach, even though I know it will work for them. That's when my wife will remind me of all the grateful attendees and memorable letters of thanks I've received over the years. She provides comfort as she helps me gain a more balanced, more realistic perspective.

Sideliners don't kick you when you're down. Unfortunately, many people do. When you're in the midst of setback or failure, many people will tell you how stupid you were or what you should have done. Others will avoid you.

By contrast, sideliners accept you even if they don't agree with you. They can see that your life might not be in the best shape, but they assume the best about you. They assume your intentions are good, even though they may disagree with your opinions and disapprove of your actions. Years ago, that's how I got through to the inmates when I worked in a juvenile reformatory. The inmates were small-time robbers, pimps, and drug dealers, and it would have been easy to lecture them about all the stupid choices they had made. What they needed, however, was someone to accept them and help them. Then they could start to make the changes they needed to make.

Sideliners don't keep track of hurts. They know that wouldn't serve any useful purpose. They know that connectedness often comes out of forgiveness. For example, I remember the story of a husband who fell asleep while driving. His wife was in the car with him when it crashed and she suffered severe injuries. When she awakened after surgery, he cried and told her how sorry he was.

"Let's not worry about it," she whispered. She took his hand and said, "I'm sure I've hurt you many times without meaning to."

Later, the wife told her friend, "I knew he didn't do it on purpose. Blaming him would have poisoned our marriage." She was a sideliner. She didn't keep track of hurts, and as a result, she went a long way toward ensuring a healthy relationship.

Sideliners take you and your dreams seriously. They don't tell you something won't work. Sideliners treat your dreams with courtesy and respect. They listen as you share your dreams, and they encourage you to pursue what's most important to you. And when asked, they offer their wisdom and guidance.

Fourth, *keep habitual critics in perspective.* Habitual critics are the people with the motto, "You can't win. You can't break even. And you can't quit." What a pain!

Keeping what these people say in perspective doesn't mean you should never listen to those who disagree with you. Not at all. Some of the best ideas come from conflict, debate, and disagreement. I'm talking about habitual critics, people who offer no positive input but are always finding faults. Be careful of putting too much stock in their opinions.

After all, habitual critics are spectators in life. They're not the players. They are disheartened people who have failed to reach a desired goal. They quit somewhere along the path of life. So they don't have the experience to advise you.

Habitual critics are disappointed, disillusioned, confused people. They hurt inside. And the only way they know how to build their lives is by trying to destroy the lives of others. Somehow or other, they think they're not so bad if other people are worse. And so they find fault, attack, and criticize—not to help, but to hurt.

You see this behavior in little kids when they call each other names. You see it when spouses continually cut each other down. And you see it when teammates find something wrong with everything somebody else suggests. These situations are poor self-esteem in action.

Thirteen-year-old Diane Luvensky of Lynn, Massachusetts, wrote about personal attacks on self-esteem in her poem, "Before the Hole Goes Through."

I saw a little boy, my brother—whom I love and accept for what he is—
showing some young children he knew a beautiful weeping willow tree, one of the wonders and beauties of nature.
Walking behind him, they were pointing and laughing, whispering and nodding—while my brother, walking, staggering but happy, had no knowledge, was unaware that they were making fun of him.
He didn't look back. The children kept laughing and giggling but he didn't see. They wouldn't have cared if he did, and he probably wouldn't have caught on.
People think that if some people are different in any way that they are like machines, that they have no feelings, need no love, need no friendship nor understanding.
But they need it even more than we, because they are constantly being rejected, left out or put down, and although it may not show at the beginning, it is wearing a hole through their hearts and we must help them before it goes all the way through.

Diane Luvensky knew that attacks and put-downs were simply a cover for poor self-esteem. And hopefully you know the same thing. Attackers may look like they've got it together. They may look like they're better or superior, but they've always got a bad case of the low-self-esteem jitters.

Finally, *don't spend too much time responding to habitual critics.* Again, that doesn't mean you should shut out all negative feedback. If you did that you would never grow. If a critic has the right intentions, by all means listen to what he or she has to say. Abraham Lincoln said, "He has a right to criticize who has a heart to help."

Just don't spend too much time and energy on the habitual critics. I learned that when I first started to write my weekly Internet newsletter, *Dr. Zimmerman's Tuesday Tips.*

Even though my newsletters are read by hundreds of thousands of people across the world every week, and even though the positive feedback has been overwhelming, I'll never forget one habitual critic. He sent me several long, highly negative e-mails.

I sat down at my computer to reply to one of his many critical letters. I really worked on my reply. I wrote and rewrote my comments. For more than an hour I carefully reworked my letter to give the kindest, most professional response I could give. And I still wasn't satisfied with my response.

Then it dawned on me. I had never spent an entire hour writing a letter to my parents, two of the most important people in the world to me. They sacrificed everything they had to make sure I had upright values, a solid education, and a chance to be more successful than they were. They never went to fancy restaurants, bought new cars, or shopped at the expensive stores. They always put my needs ahead of their wants.

I had not spent so much time writing to two of the dearest people I know. And here I was sweating over how to respond to a habitual critic. I realized I was a fool. I threw away the letter and went on to some higher priorities. I learned, once again, that what other people say about you is not as important in life as what you believe about yourself. And believing in yourself is so much easier when you hang around the "right" people. Choose your connections carefully.

Concluding Thoughts

Other people cannot give you your self-esteem. And they cannot make you have a positive attitude. That's the result of the choices you make.

But if you hang around the right people, maintaining your self-esteem is a great deal easier. And if you learn to respond to people in the right way, building your positive attitude is also a great deal easier.

The wife of one of my speaking colleagues illustrated this. She and her husband had fallen on hard times financially. They were going under. So her husband decided to push his boss for a raise, a risky move that might have resulted in his termination. But he took the risk, and to his delight he got an immediate raise.

When the husband returned home that evening, he told his wife the good news. She was thrilled and prepared an extra-special dinner. They both wanted to celebrate.

As the man sat down for dinner, he noticed a piece of paper on his plate. His wife had written him a note that read, "I knew you'd get the raise. You deserved it. This dinner will tell you how much I love you."

Later that evening, as the man was walking to another room, he saw another piece of paper that had apparently fallen out of his wife's pocket. It said, "Don't worry about not getting the raise. You deserved it anyway. This dinner will tell you much I love you." His wife had been prepared to give support no matter what the outcome.

People like that make it easier for you to build and maintain your positive attitude. Make sure you find some, and then spend some time with them.

RELATIONSHIP EXERCISES

1. Choose Your Sideliners

a. List three people who serve as sideliners in your life, or list three people you would like to have as sideliners.

b. Make sure these people appear on your schedule on a regular basis. Don't leave it to chance. If they are not already a part of your routine, start to see them or talk to them at least once a month.

2. Your Positive-People Network*

1. Understanding Your Present Network
   a. Think of all the people that you know and interact with—friends, co-workers, close family members, relatives, church acquaintances, neighbors, clients, association colleagues, service people, and competitors. All these relationships serve a purpose or meet some need for you.
   b. Write the names of people you go to when you
      1. Have a problem
      2. Want to learn new things
      3. Want personal acceptance, approval, and/or emotional support
      4. Want to have fun
      5. Want good, sound advice
      6. Want someone to listen intently to whatever is on your mind
      7. Want some honest feedback
      8. Want professional appreciation/recognition for your skills and your accomplishments

---

*Adapted from the work of Dr. Donald A. Tubesing, *Personal Recharging: Rx for Burnout in the Workplace*, published by Whole Person Associates, Inc., 1981.

2. Examining your positive-people network
   a. Look over your list. Who fills these needs for you? One person? Several people? Different people at different times? What are your conclusions?
   b. Does one person's name appear over and over again? Do you rely on that person for too many things? What are your conclusions? Don't expect one person to function as your entire support network.
3. Growing your positive-people network
   a. Understanding your support network
      1. Look for holes in your network. Are there some needs in section 1b where you have no one listed? Or very few people?
      2. Don't pick the wrong people. You'll get frustrated if you pick the wrong people to meet certain needs. For example, don't expect your "professional appreciation" need to be met by a boss who never recognizes anyone.
   b. Fixing the holes
      1. As you grow and change, some holes may appear in your network. Some people who were supportive at one stage may not be able to help you in your next phase of growth. So it is important to reevaluate your support network regularly.
      2. Look at your list again and put an asterisk next to the areas (section 1b) where you would like to enhance your network.
      3. In the space below, write the names of people who might become part of your positive-people network.
      4. Write your plan for nurturing connectedness with people who are already in your network and those you want to include.
      5. Make mail, phone, or face-to-face contact with at least one of these people every week.

CHAPTER SIX

Enthusiasm

FAKE IT 'TIL YOU MAKE IT

The Power of Enthusiasm

A sixty-year-old man was planning to retire shortly, so he set three goals for his future. He wanted to play more golf, travel to more places, and spend more time with his grandchildren.

His plan was great—with one exception. The man didn't have any grandchildren. He had four adult children, all married, but no one was reproducing.

When they all got together for Christmas dinner, he said, "I'll be retiring soon. I've set three goals for retirement, and I want to share them with you. I want to play more golf, travel a bit more, and spend more time with my grandchildren."

He continued, "As you know, I don't have any grandchildren. So today I want to make this announcement. I've established a one million dollar trust fund that will be given to the first couple who blesses me with a grandchild. Now, let's bow our heads and thank the Lord for dinner."

He bowed his head and prayed, then opened his eyes and the room was empty. He immediately saw the power of enthusiasm!

Few forces on Earth are more powerful than enthusiasm. Indeed, the very word "enthusiasm" comes from the Greek word "entheos," which literally means being "filled with God." Enthusiasm is an almost supernatural source of power.

In fact, the Scottish physicist Sir Edward V. Appleton said his enthusiasm helped him win the Nobel Prize. According to him, it was the secret of his amazing achievements. He added, "I rate enthusiasm even above professional skill."

Charles M. Schwab, the great industrialist, concurred. He said, "A person can succeed at anything for which there is enthusiasm."

And Henry Ford said, "Enthusiasm is the yeast that makes your hope rise to the stars . . . the sparkle in your eye . . . the swing in your gait, the grip in your hand, the irresistible surge of your will, and your energy to execute your ideas. Enthusiasts are fighters. They have fortitude. They have staying qualities."

They all seemed to say that enthusiasm is a special kind of energy that allows you to keep going. But enthusiasm also helps you to bounce back when you hit bottom. Author H. W. Arnold noted, "The worst bankrupt is the man who has lost his enthusiasm. Let a man lose everything in the world but his enthusiasm and he will come through again to success."

Best of all, enthusiasm is an energy that jumps from person to person. In fact, living or working with an enthusiastic person without catching some of her energy is almost impossible. As Emory Ward said, "Enthusiasm, like measles, mumps, and the common cold, is highly contagious."

The good news is that you can be enthusiastic all the time. And the more enthusiastic you are, the more positive your attitude will be. The two go hand in hand.

So how can you get that kind of enthusiasm? Through the actions you take.

ACT AS IF

In Act III of *Hamlet,* Shakespeare said, "Assume a virtue, if you have it not." In other words, if you want to *be* a certain kind of person, you have to *behave* that way.

Several hundred years later, Dr. William James confirmed Shakespeare's insight. As one of the founding fathers of modern psychology, Dr. James spent his entire professional life researching the subject of motivation and attitude. He concluded, "If you want a quality, act as if you already had it."

This technique works for any personality trait you might want to have. If, for example, you want to be more patient, force yourself to act patiently, even if your guts are churning inside, and eventually you will feel and be more patient.

The same goes for enthusiasm and a positive attitude. If you want more enthusiasm, you can't wait until the problems of life are all gone. That will never happen. Having no problems means you're dead. Simply start acting enthusiastically and you will become more enthusiastic. As Dr. George W. Crane puts it, "Act the way you'd like to be and soon you'll be the way you act."

BE AN ACTOR, NOT A REACTOR

The columnist Sydney Harris gave a great illustration of this principle. He wrote about visiting a friend in downtown Manhattan. As they walked to a newspaper stand, Sydney could see that the man selling the papers was negative. He was grouchy, antagonistic, and yelling at people. But Sydney's friend said very nicely, "Good morning, Charlie. How are you doing? Good to see you!"

The salesman growled back at him.

The friend said, "Oh, I see." He picked up the paper, paid for it and said, "Thanks a lot, Charlie. I always get great service. I appreciate that!"

The salesman growled again.

As they walked away, Sydney noticed that his friend turned back and said, "Now, Charlie, come on. Smile. Have a good day. See you tomorrow. Bye-bye."

The salesman growled a third time.

Sydney was confused by the entire situation. So as they walked home, he asked his friend, "Does that salesman always act so rudely?"

His friend replied, "Yes, every day."

"And do you always treat him that nicely?" Sydney wondered.

His friend said, "Yes, of course."

So Sydney asked, "Why? Why do you treat him so nicely when that's the way he treats you all the time?"

His friend responded with this marvelous answer: "I don't want him to decide how I'm going to behave. I'm an actor, not a reactor."

Sydney's friend's response held tremendous wisdom. Anybody can react to somebody else's negativity and come down to their level. But the truly mature individual—or the person working on his or her attitude—chooses to *act* instead. They fake it until they make it.

What about you? Are you more the actor or the reactor? Do you behave positively and enthusiastically most of the time? Or are you a bit more moody, going up and down in your feelings?

F. W. Woolworth took on the role of an actor early on in his business career. When he was about to open a store and start his new business, a merchant down the street ran an ad in the local paper that read: "Do your local shopping here. We have been in business for fifty years!"

Young Woolworth was concerned and feared he could not compete. Then he decided to be an actor instead of a reactor. He ran his own ad the following week that read: "We've been in business only one week. All of our merchandise is brand new."

Many people would have been immobilized in that situation. They would have reacted with fear, and they would have remained stuck in their negative emotions. And many people live their lives as reactors. They react to the day of the week, thinking, "Ugh. It's Monday." They react to the weather, saying, "Oh, darn, it's cold outside" . . . or snowing, or raining, or cloudy. Or they react to the report from Wall Street: "My, my, my . . . It's up . . . it's down." All of which, of course, are lousy ways to live!

If you're more of a reactor, I have some good news for you. You can overcome your reactive tendencies and become an actor. You can *be* more enthusiastic if you will just *behave* more enthusiastically. Just practice the following six skills, and when you do, you will have more energy and a more positive attitude than ever before.

1. Do Not Catch the Other Person's Disease

You may think that behaving enthusiastically is not easy. After all, you may be underpaid and underappreciated at work. You may have to work with some real tough customers. You may be disrespected at home. And you may receive unfair criticism from others.

That's life. But you can still control your life by refusing to catch the other person's disease. You can refuse to buy into their negativity.

If you're a manager, for example, and you have a number of complaining, negative people on your staff, you must refuse to come down to their level. Indeed, if you did give in to their negativity, you would lose all your power to motivate them, and you would lose your own positive attitude.

If you're married and your spouse gets crabby at you, you know better than to get crabby back. Indeed, if you did, you'd have a fight on your hands.

Do not catch the other person's disease. I learned the importance of this when I served as a professor. On occasion, a few of my students would ask such things as, "Do you take attendance?" "Do we have to come to class every day?" "Will that be on the test?" "Do I have to take notes?" and "If I'm gone the next three days, will I miss anything?" Their questions reflected negativity towards learning. I knew that if I caught their negativity I would lose all my power to get them excited about the subject.

Refuse, reject, and resist the negativity of others. You'll see quite a bit of it if you choose to be an actor instead of a reactor. Negative people do not like the positive attitude they see in others.

For example, one of my bosses told me years ago that he got a little sick and tired of my cheerful "Good mornings" at the office each day. He said, "We don't all feel that way."

And one of my former students talked about the huge promotion she received and her enthusiastic response to the good news. Later, she was told by her manager that her response was unprofessional.

You've got to be careful. Even though you may be tempted and pushed to become like the negative folks around you, you must not catch their disease. As Anatole France said so well, "I prefer the folly of enthusiasm to the indifference of wisdom."

You may have to practice this skill. I know I had to. I used to walk down the hallways of the university in the morning, greeting colleagues and students. Almost everybody I encountered would respond with their own upbeat greeting. But two professors never once in seven years responded. No hellos, smiles, or comments. They walked right by.

Do you ever meet people like that? It would be very easy to catch their disease, and it would be very easy to think, "Forget it! How many years do I have to be positive to get some response out of those people?" I know I thought that way sometimes.

But then I reminded myself that I am an actor, not a reactor. I did not know what difficulties those negative, nonresponsive professors faced, but I did know that I would not take my cues from them.

To build your enthusiasm and condition your attitude to be more positive, do not catch the other person's disease.

2. Say Something Positive to Everyone

Just like you don't have to be enthusiastic to behave enthusiastically, in a similar sense, you don't have to feel positive to say something positive.

Enthusiastic people always have an optimistic greeting, a cheery "Good morning," or a friendly "Hello." They always have something positive to share. They do not restrict their positive communication to those times when they're in the mood or when they feel like it.

Like everybody else, enthusiastic people have negative feelings or problems once in a while. And they talk about those things on occasion. But they also know that when they least feel like saying something positive, they most need to do it. As they say positive things to other people, they are acting enthusiastically, and they end up feeling that way.

And so do the other people around them. The great football coach Vince Lombardi knew that. When he came to the Green Bay Packers, he faced a defeated, dispirited team. He stood before them and said, "Gentlemen, we are going to have a great football team. We are going to win games. You are going to learn to block. You are going to learn to run. You are going to learn to tackle. You are going to outplay the teams that come against you."

Lombardi continued, "And how is this to be done? You are to have confidence in me and enthusiasm for my system. The secret of the whole matter will be what goes on in your head. Hereafter, I want you to think of only three things: your home, your religion, and the Green Bay Packers, in that order!"

The players sat up in their chairs, totally captivated by Lombardi's enthusiasm. Indeed, the quarterback later said, "I walked out of that meeting feeling ten feet tall!" And that year the Packers won seven games with virtually all the same players who had lost ten games the year before. The next year they won a division title and the third year the Super Bowl.

How would you rate yourself in terms of staying positive toward other people? How would your boss, coworkers, customers, friends, and family members rate you?

Of course, saying positive things to positive people is easier than saying them to negative people. But that's not how this particular skill works. If you're trying to be more enthusiastic, if you want a more positive attitude, you need to say something genuinely positive even to the most difficult of people.

A waitress named Becky in Bowling Green, Kentucky showed me that. As I sat in a restaurant early one morning, working on a speech that I would give later that day, Becky came over to me, filled with enthusiasm. She clapped her hands together and said, "Oh, good morning, sir. It's a great day to be alive, and you're a good-looking one, honey! What do you want for breakfast?"

I put down my notes, gave my order, and then watched her go from table to table, cheering up the whole place. People were laughing, joking, and interacting. Her enthusiasm was spreading to everyone—with the exception of one man.

The man had a grouchy expression on his unshaven face. He smoked one cigarette after another as he gulped down his coffee and eggs. I watched Becky as she approached him. In her same enthusiastic voice she said, "Isn't this a wonderful day? You've got to start it right, honey. What else can I get for you? I wouldn't want you to go away hungry."

He glared at her and asked gruffly, "What's so darn good about this so-called wonderful day?"

Becky was taken a bit off guard, but she wasn't deflated. She just stood there, silent for two or three seconds, and then answered, "Well, if you missed a few days, sir, you'd find out how precious every day is!" She had learned how to stay enthusiastic by saying positive things to the people she met. And you can learn the same kind of skill.

When you speak the positive to other people, you will discover that you can't help but feel more enthusiastic yourself. And one of two things will happen when you are around negative people: they will pick up some of your enthusiasm, or at the very least, they will not succeed in pulling you down to their level.

3. Practice Positive Expectations

If you expect bad things to happen, they often do. You'll find something to complain about. But if you expect good things to happen, more often than not, good things seem to take place. So the third way you can become more enthusiastic is to manage your expectations. Practice positive expectations. Create your own self-fulfilling prophecy. I can see the power of expectation working in my own life. I'm usually happy and enthusiastic, but not always. When I get down, I ask myself, *Why am I not happy today? Why am I not enthusiastic?* Almost always, the problem can be traced to a negative expectation: I'm not looking forward to anything. I'm just putting in my time, thinking, "Another day, another dollar."

But when I'm practicing positive expectations, when I'm look-ing forward to something, my entire attitude, my outlook, and my energy are changed for the better. I could be looking forward to meeting a friend for lunch next week, or spending a weekend with my wife at a bed-and-breakfast. But the anticipation of positive experiences keeps me from losing my positive attitude.

What kind of expectations do you carry around? Are you looking forward to good things about to happen? Or do you fear the worst? W. Clement Stone, the multimillionaire insurance magnate, was known for expecting the best and for being an "inverse paranoid." He believed the world was plotting to do him good. When he sent an insurance salesman into Iowa, for example, the salesman came back totally depressed and discouraged. He said it was impossible to sell insurance in Iowa because there were too many Amish people, and they were all clannish. Stone replied, "Great. When you sell one, you sell them all."

But the salesman said the Amish were tight with their money. Again Stone replied, "Great. They know the value of money, and they'll want to protect it with insurance."

Are you rich in expectations? You need to examine them very carefully. Dr. Norman Vincent Peale said, "There is another kind of poverty—one that most people never think about—and it's the poverty of expectations." In other words, if you're not getting what you'd like, it may be because your expectations are too low.

Of course, you may have been trained to have low or negative expectations. You may have been taught to think, "If you don't expect much, you won't be disappointed when you don't get much." But that's the problem. By not expecting much you rule out any chance of winning. I prefer the author Goethe's approach. He said, "In all things it is better to hope than despair."

When you practice positive expectations, you keep your enthusiasm high and your attitude positive. My daughter and I learned that lesson together. Like any normal child, she did not want to get out of bed in the morning. In fact, getting her out of bed often turned into a fight.

So I decided to try this enthusiasm skill on her. I practiced positive expectations. One day, I went into her bedroom, clapped my hands together, and said, "Hey, sweetie, something good is going to happen to you today."

She jumped up and said, "What? What?"

I said, "I don't know, but I know something good is going to happen. I want you to look for it and give me a report at the end of the day." She groaned.

When she returned from school later that day, I reminded her that something good was going to happen to her and asked her what happened. She replied, "Nothing. It was the worst day of my life." She was being melodramatic, to say the least.

I said, "I'm sorry. Let me see if I can understand. Maybe your friends wouldn't play with you during recess. That would feel bad." That wasn't it; she played hopscotch and jumped rope with them that day.

I tried again, "Maybe your teacher made fun of you in class. That would feel bad." That wasn't it either; she got three answers right and got a gold star.

"Then maybe you weren't allowed to have lunch today; you had to sit in the cafeteria while the other kids ate." That wasn't it either; they had spaghetti and lots of sauce. It was wonderful.

Obviously my first attempt at using or infusing positive expectations didn't seem to work. But I kept at it. Every morning for three weeks, I repeated the same routine. I would go into her bedroom, clap my hands, and tell her something good was going to happen. And I would ask her about the good when she returned from school—all with little or no results.

But the fourth week it clicked. She came home from school one day and asked how many good things happened to *me* that day! She had four and began to list them. And for a long time afterwards we played a little game to see who could find the most positives during a particular day. We had both learned to be actors instead of reactors.

Again, are you expecting good things to happen? Are you looking forward to today, this weekend, next week, next month, next year, or five years from now? The more things you look forward to, the stronger your enthusiasm will be.

4. Use the Positive "But"

By now you've probably learned that a positive attitude won't necessarily prevent problems from coming into your life. But a positive attitude prevents them from staying in your life. And one of the best ways to do that is to use the positive "but."

In simple terms, counteract every negative in your life with something positive. Neutralize the negative. Change your focus.

I teach the participants in my Peak Performance Boot Camp how to do that by drawing a line down the middle of a sheet of paper. At the top of the left side, I ask them to write the word *Problems*, and then list all their problems in that column. On the right- hand side, I ask them to write the word *Blessings*. I then challenge them to counteract every problem with a blessing.

One participant wrote this: "I lost my wife to cancer . . . *but* I still have my three children. I lost a lot of money when my business partner embezzled our funds . . . *but* I still have the loyalty of my customers. I've gained weight . . . *but* I have the motivation to do something about it. My son moved out of town . . . *but* he still calls me every week."

Do you see the point? That man could have focused on the fact that he lost his wife, lost some money, gained some weight, and missed his son. And he would have been miserable. But when he focused on the fact that he has children, customers, motivation, and contact, he was able to maintain his positive attitude.

That's exactly how attitude works. You can focus on your problems, or you can focus on your blessings. And what you choose to focus on makes all the difference in the world.

What kinds of problems are you having in your life? Are you applying the positive "but" to them?

Susan Duxter did. She talked of being beaten and robbed in the Dominican Republic, which was negative. But forever after, she found herself telling her family at least five times a day how much she loved them. She had rarely told them before. They all became a great deal closer. Indeed, Susan said if she had known that her worst experience would have become her best experience, "I would have paid them to rob me."

Thomas Edison was also a proponent of the positive "but." One time he shocked his friends who were despairing over his deafness. Edison responded that it was true that he was deaf, but on the other hand, his deafness was his greatest blessing. It saved him from having to listen to others tell him why things couldn't be done.

Actress Molly Picon used the positive "but" when she heard her fellow performers complain about the accommodations on tour. Molly said, "I never complain about such things. My grandmother raised eleven children in four rooms."

"How did she manage?" someone asked.

"Easy," Molly replied. "She took in boarders."

You see, anyone can tell you how tough times are. Anybody can see what was lost. But it takes brains to see what remains.

To have more enthusiasm, to have a more positive attitude, counteract every negative in your life with a positive "but." Actors do it all the time.

5. Find Reasons to Celebrate

Life isn't black or white, good or bad. No matter how rotten a situation is, personally or professionally, you can always find a reason to celebrate. If you can find the reason, and if you take a moment to celebrate, you will maintain your enthusiasm.

The poet Emily Dickinson had a father who practiced this skill. One evening in Amherst, Massachusetts, he hurried to the church and began to pull the bell rope urgently. Hearing the bell, the villagers rushed from their homes, wondering what had happened. Was there a fire? An accident? Some tragedy they should know about? None of that. Mr. Dickinson was simply overcome by the beauty of the sunset, and he was summoning everyone so they could enjoy it as well.

You can always find something to celebrate. Author Frank Tillipaugh addressed this in his book *The Church Unleashed*. He noted that soldiers on the front line do not complain about petty things such as the food they're eating. They're just glad they're alive and can eat. By contrast, a few miles back of the front lines, complaining is the norm.

Are you finding reasons to celebrate? And are you celebrating often enough? You don't have to wait for the good times or the easy times to celebrate. Colonel Chuck Scott taught me that. During the Carter administration, a few dozen Americans were held hostage in Iran for 444 days. Of all the hostages, Colonel Scott was the highest ranking military official, and as a result, he was tortured more than anyone else.

Sometime after the hostages were released, I shared the platform with Colonel Scott. We were both speaking to IBM. I was totally captivated by his stories of torture and interrogation, but more than anything else, I was blown away by his comment that his experience in Iran was the greatest experience of his lifetime.

He went on to explain that his captivity gave him reasons to celebrate. Even though he would never want to be tortured again, he realized that if he could make it through Iran, he could make it through anything.

As a result of his experiences, Scott says he no longer worries what people think about him, because he can always make new friends. He doesn't worry about money, because he can always start over again. He doesn't worry about the weather, because he's alive to live in it. He found reasons to celebrate his terrifying experience, and that in turn has given him a great deal of peace.

As I've said, you can always find something to celebrate. You may have an extremely irritating coworker, for example. In fact, your coworker may be so difficult that you decide to read a book on dealing with difficult people. You could practice your newfound skills on your coworker and turn the whole thing into a positive learning experience. Then you have a reason to celebrate.

Of course, you can celebrate for many reasons and in many ways. But I recommend Dr. Ira A. Greenberg's approach. As the head of the Behavioral Studies Institute, he urges people to succeed at something every day. Dr. Greenberg said, "Each day, do something you can be proud of. Each night take pleasure in remembering it."

Today, start looking and start counting. List your reasons for celebrating.

6. Do It Now

One of the quickest ways to lose your enthusiasm is to sit on the good ideas that come your way. In fact, having a positive attitude is almost impossible if you don't implement some of your good ideas. You've got to do it now. As Mae West said, "He who hesitates is last."

For example, you may think of calling a friend from college that you haven't spoken to in years. But then you decide you're too busy right now, and two years pass before you make that call. Or you decide to write your aunt because you feel out of touch with her. But then you get distracted by something, and another month goes by. Or while reminiscing about high school you think about a teacher who really made a difference in your life, and consider writing a note of thanks. Then you decide she probably doesn't remember you, and the idea slips away. In all such instances, you simply cannot feel good about yourself, putting your good ideas on hold or letting them pass away.

You've got to do it now. Take action.

One of my seminar attendees did exactly that, and he reported some wonderful results. He decided to contact the teacher who had made the biggest difference in his life. Indeed, without her, he said he probably would have wound up in prison, for he was dealing drugs, stealing money, and vandalizing property as a teenager.

Today he works as an executive in a big corporation, makes lots of money, and is very successful. So he went back to his high school and asked about his favorite teacher. He got her address and wrote a note, telling her how she had changed his life. At the time, he didn't know if she would ever get the note, or if she would remember him.

Two weeks later he received a response from her. The note said, "I'm in a nursing home, living alone, in my eighties. My mind is clear, but my body needs special care. That's why I'm here. I taught for over fifty years in the public school system, but your note of appreciation thrilled me as nothing has in years. I'm so glad to know that I made a difference in your life. I believed in you then, and I still believe in you. Thanks for writing."

He was happy to know that his note cheered his teacher. But the bigger lesson, he told me, was the importance of taking action on his good ideas. He not only made her feel better, but he made himself feel better. It was a tremendous boost to his level of enthusiasm.

How good are you at taking action on your good ideas? Do you tend to do it now? Or do you tend to procrastinate?

The End Result: A Determined Actor

If you practice these six skills, you will become a determined actor. You will be able to cope when the tough times come, and you will be able to maintain your enthusiastic, positive attitude.

And there will be tough times. You will experience challenges to your attitude. You may have to work with negative people, and you may be living with negative people. But in the final analysis, it's not so much how people act around you or treat you that makes the biggest difference in life; it's how you condition yourself to respond.

Let me contrast two individuals to illustrate what I mean. The first individual had no particular problems, but she was terribly distraught. And the other person had every conceivable problem but had lots of enthusiasm. The difference came in their conditioning.

The first person was one of my freshmen advisees at the university where I taught. Unlike my other advisees, who typically came in for their one obligatory meeting, Kay came to my office ten times during fall quarter. And every time she came, she would cry and cry and cry. I would ask her what the problem was, and every week she would talk about how worried she was about her grades. She didn't think she was smart enough for college.

But Kay was valedictorian of her high school class, and she had had great college entrance scores. I kept encouraging her, telling her that she could do it, but she continued to worry and cry.

At the end of the quarter, she came into my office and showed off her straight A's. I thought, "Thank goodness. That problem is solved." But she returned to my office every week of winter quarter, still worried and crying. She was afraid she wouldn't be able to maintain her grades!

Obviously, Kay had all the talent she needed to do well academically. She had no problems in that area, but she also had no confidence or enthusiasm. She had never practiced the six skills in this chapter, and she had never learned how to be a determined actor.

My father, in contrast, saw every kind of problem you can think of, yet maintained his enthusiasm. He lost his father to cancer after months of caring for him. Two years after he lost his dad, he found his wife dead at fifty-two years of age. Two months later, he lost his job and couldn't find another one. And then two years later, he lost his brother to cancer.

In all that tragedy, I never saw him lose his enthusiasm for life. He joined a group for widowed, divorced, and single people. He started dating again, and it wasn't too long before he met a person he liked a great deal and married her.

After two weeks of marriage, they began wondering what they could do with their new lives. They had no jobs and money was scarce, but they were both determined actors. And they decided to take action.

They bought a few hundred Christmas trees, rented a space, and went into business. They used some of the proceeds for their living expenses, and they invested some of the money into land where they could raise their own Christmas trees. They did so well that they began shipping trees to their customers across the country, and they've taken their free time to travel the world.

When I look at Kay and then at my father, the contrast is huge. I'm reminded once again that attitude makes the difference. And with practice, you can have an unshakable positive attitude. You can become the determined actor you need to be.

Dr. Hans Selye confirmed that. A physician and the leading researcher on stress management, Selye wrote, "I now believe life is 10 percent what happens to you and 90 percent how you condition yourself to respond."

What condition are you in? Are you in good shape, ready to handle any problem or challenge thrown your way? Or are you out of shape? Just like an athlete who needs conditioning to compete and win, you need to condition yourself as well. So work on your attitude and work on your enthusiasm. The two go hand in hand.

A Parting Thought

Years ago, the American philosopher Ralph Waldo Emerson said, "Nothing great was ever achieved without enthusiasm." He was right. Enthusiasm is the energy behind every success. And with enough enthusiastic energy, you never have to be frightened by those who seem to have more talent than you, because in the end energy will prevail.

Jeffrey Archer said it best. In his book *Take It From Me,* Archer wrote, "Energy plus talent and you are a king; energy and no talent and you are still a prince; talent and no energy and you are a pauper."

Practice the skills in this chapter, and you will gain all the enthusiastic energy you need to be the king or queen—or at least the prince or princess—of your life.

ENTHUSIASM EXERCISES

1. Self-exploration Questions

In groups of two or three, discuss your responses to the following questions. Or, if you're alone, write out your responses to the questions.

a. Skill 1: Do not catch the other person's disease. When you are around negative people, how susceptible are you? How likely are you to catch some of their negativity? Do you join in the conversation, adding a few negative comments of your own? Does your mood sour for the day? Or are you immune to their negativity?

b. Skill 2: Say something positive to everyone. On a scale of one to ten, with ten being the best, how would you score yourself on this skill? Explain.

c. Skill 3: Practice positive expectations. How consistently do you practice positive expectations? What positive expectations do you have in your life right now?

d. Skill 4: Use the positive 'but.' How often do you neutralize the negative situations in your life by focusing on something positive instead? How could you improve your use of this skill?

e. Skill 5: Find reasons to celebrate. How do others see you? Do they see a person who is always filled with good news or bad news? Do they see a person who can find something good in almost any situation? Or do they see a person who focuses on what has gone wrong and will go wrong?

f. Skill 6: Do it now. How good are you at activating good ideas? Do you get right on them? Or do you put them off? How could you improve your follow-through and implementation of good ideas?

2. Enthusiasm Practice

a. There's an old psychological truth that states, "We do not sing because we are happy; we are happy because we sing." In other words, action precedes feeling. What actions could you take to kick your enthusiasm into gear? Perhaps you could sing, whistle, smile, skip, or dance. Hundreds of possibilities exist. List ten that you could take.

b. Spend two minutes a day, twice a day, to practice one of the actions you listed.

CHAPTER SEVEN

Discipline

YOU CANNOT CLIMB UPHILL
BY THINKING DOWNHILL THOUGHTS

A New Diet

By now, you're probably convinced that few things are more important to your success than developing an unshakable positive attitude. You would probably agree with Dale Carnegie, who said, "Happiness doesn't depend upon who you are or what you have; it depends on what you think." And you've read my review of Dr. Martin Seligman's research, where he found that successful people think twice as many positive thoughts as negative ones.

Of course, the challenge comes in the work that has to be done. How do you get to think that way and keep thinking that way? How do you get in shape and stay in shape when it comes to the area of positive attitudes? I've found a "positive attitude diet" that works for me and will work for you.

Like any other diet, the positive attitude diet is all about feeding yourself the right foods in the right proportions. After all, what you feed your body determines to a large extent the kind of body you will have. And the same truth applies to your mind.

In addition, like any other diet, you must also follow a plan. You need to be consistent in following the diet if you expect the right kind of outcome.

So what are the right foods and what is the right plan? I call it the Seven-Day Mental Diet. All you have to do is write the seven strategies on seven different cards, and then carry one of the cards with you each day. Think about that strategy throughout the day, and whenever you do, practice the strategy for a few seconds. You'll get an immediate benefit.

Repeat that approach, focusing on a different strategy the next day. After you've gotten through all seven days, start the whole process over again. Just keep on doing this, and you will not only have a positive attitude, you will release the power of a positive attitude into all parts of your life.

The Seven-Day Mental Diet is simple and it works. All you have to do is follow it.

DAY ONE: FEED YOUR MIND

Instead of living your life on autopilot, letting any and all thoughts come into your mind, consciously feed your mind positive input. Feed your mind all the positive input you can give it. Read inspirational stories of people who have overcome great difficulties. Subscribe to "good news" magazines. And read spiritually uplifting devotionals. On the first day of every week, take a few minutes throughout the day to read inspirational material.

In addition to reading positive materials, listening to positive recordings is another great way to fill your mind with the fuel it needs. And fortunately, this approach is very easy. Thousands and thousands of hours of great motivational, educational, and religious material are available on tape, CDs, and a host of other formats. In fact, never in history has so much good material been available to so many people in such a user-friendly format.

Personally, I own hundreds, maybe thousands of tapes and CDs of great talks that I've heard. And I take time to listen to those kinds of things every day, for at least ten minutes a day, like taking my daily vitamins. I even listen to some of the same recordings over and over again, because I know that it takes several exposures to the same material before it is totally assimilated.

Of course you're wondering if listening to motivational material works. You bet! Companies often report that their top salespeople listen to positive, motivational, inspirational recordings every single day of their lives. One sales manager said, "They don't listen because they are the best. They are the best because they listen."

It's true. As someone who has been a professor, professional speaker, and consultant during my adult life, I've seen it over and over again. The top people in every job and every profession are the ones who buy the recordings. They're the ones who listen. And they're the ones who show up for the motivational seminars and listen most intently.

The losers, on the other hand, resist all such activity. They may have twenty different excuses for not reading and listening to positive materials. Some of those negative people say it costs too much money to buy all those motivational materials. Yet those same people will find the money to pay for cable TV and junk food. They'll spend money on an insurance policy that covers their homes, but they won't insure their minds or their futures with a more positive attitude.

The average person, for example, spends about $500 a year on the outside of his or her head, getting haircuts, applying shampoos, and using makeup. But the average person spends about $50 educating the inside of his head. That's just plain crazy. A person's mind is the one thing that will make a difference in a person's life, but the average person won't read ten positive books or listen to ten positive recordings in his or her entire lifetime.

Other folks say they're too busy to read and listen. What a flimsy excuse. Many people spend five years of their lives driving back and forth to work and two years of their lives eating. So they could find some time to feed their minds—if they really wanted to.

For example, you could reduce your TV viewing by a few minutes a day and take those few minutes to read some good positive materials. Or you could use your driving time as your positivity "feeding time." Just pop a recording into your CD player as you commute to work each day. Do the same thing on the way home. It will prepare you for a productive day at work and meaningful time at home. And over time, it will change your life for the better.

Are you feeding your mind? Are you reading lots of positive motivational materials? Are you listening to motivational recordings on a regular basis? Or are you "too busy" or "too broke" to invest in yourself?

Starting your week with the positive will give you a huge release of power, life, and beauty—just like what happened to an area of Texas that hadn't seen rain in seven years. The ground had baked to the point where deep cracks formed in the earth. No plants could grow on the dusty, dry surface.

Then it rained. Seven inches of rain soaked the dead soil in twenty-four hours. Finally, beautiful bluebonnet flowers began to emerge from the barren earth, and soon the ground was covered with life.

Power and beauty were in the dry, cracked earth all the time, but it took the rain to bring it out. The same is true for you. Flood your mind with positive input at least once a week, and you'll be amazed at all the good things that come out of you.

Even though my diet plan says you should feed your mind on Day One, you can accelerate your diet. If you want better results or quicker results, feed your mind some positive input *every* day. It will make a huge difference.

DAY TWO: SEE ALL THE GOOD AROUND YOU

On Day Two, open your mind to all the wonderful things that happen around you. See all the good things. Take time to notice and appreciate them. This can be as simple as finding something beautiful in nature. As Dr. David Bouda, assistant professor of oncology at the University of Nebraska College of Medicine in Omaha, said, "I've never heard anyone looking at a rainbow say, 'Gee, I wish it had more blue and a little less red.'"

You can see all the good around you in three ways. First, *establish some positive triggers.* Positive people live in the same world that negative people do. They both get exposed to thousands of words, images, and situations every day, and oftentimes they get exposed to the same things. The difference is that many positive people have established some triggers that ignite a positive response inside themselves.

A trigger is nothing more than a reminder, something small that reminds a person to think or be positive. Some people, for example, carry a little cross or other religious symbol in their pockets. Whenever they reach in and feel it, they're reminded of the positive benefits of their faith.

Some people look for smiles. Whenever they see someone smiling on the street, in a passing car, or down the hallway at work, they put a smile on their face.

Other people use such things as landmarks or radio commercials. Whenever they pass a certain landmark on the way to work, or whenever they hear a commercial, they look for something good around them. It really doesn't matter what kind of triggers you establish, just as long as you use them.

Second, *keep a journal of the good*. Write down fifty wonderful things that happen to you on Day Two. Include everything, even the smallest things—such as finding a quarter on the sidewalk or receiving a cheery "Good morning" from a stranger on the street.

"After a while," according to Dr. Susan Jeffers, author of *End the Struggle and Dance with Life*, "you'll realize that most things that happen are positive, and you don't have to dwell on the negative." And the negative things won't seem so important.

Third, *look for the good in every situation*. Something good exists in every situation, no matter how difficult it might seem, personally or professionally. If you can see the good, you're doing exactly what you should be doing on Day Two of this diet.

I watched my wife do this a few years ago. She spent seven days a week, twenty-fours a day, for four months, caring for her mother as she died of cancer. It was an extremely difficult burden because her mother had never been an easy, warm, or loving individual. But one time during that four-month vigil, her mother turned to her and said she loved her. It was the first and only time in her entire sixty-eight years of life that my wife's mother had ever said these words to her daughter. And this became the good that my wife was able to see in this painful situation.

One of my daughters has also learned to see the good in every situation. When she was six years old, our family was going through a tough situation, and it came out in her griping. In fact, for a period of time, she seemed to be griping almost constantly. She was saying, "Life is dumb," "I don't like school," "I don't like my teacher," "I haven't got any good friends," "I haven't got any nice toys," and "Life is boring."

One day, while driving her home from school, she started another tirade of complaints. And I became fed up. So I lectured her on looking for the good in every situation. I told her, "I'm sick of all your negative comments. Life isn't that bad. Look for the good from now on, and tell me that."

Just as I said that, a train stopped, blocking our way. She looked at me and said, "Ha! What's so good about that?"

I didn't know. But I learned a long time ago as a teacher that I could always say, "Why don't you think about it for a little while and maybe you can think of the answer?"

She sat quietly in the front seat of the car with me, deep in thought for a few minutes. And then said, "Oh, I know what's good about this! I get to talk to you a bit longer." Of course she was right. On a normal afternoon I would have gone into the house and done some work, while she would have gone outside and played. But that day we had some extra time to talk—because she saw the good in our situation.

Something good is always happening around you. On Day Two, look extra hard and make sure you notice those good things.

DAY THREE: SPEAK WORDS OF GRATITUDE

On Days One and Two of the diet, you're feeding your mind the positive, and you're seeing the positive around you. On Day Three, it's time to let some of it out. Give thanks. Speak words of gratitude.

Whether you say it out loud or think the thoughts, whether you tell someone face to face or say it privately in your prayers, whether you share it at a staff meeting or write it in your newsletter, you need to verbalize your thankfulness. In fact, this is one of the best things you can do for yourself, as well as for those around you. Thankfulness lifts your spirits and builds your relationships. And that's why a great deal of truth exists in the old maxim "Money doesn't buy happiness, but thankfulness will."

For some people, this will be an easy day on the diet. You're already into giving thanks. For others, this may be a challenge. You may think you have too many difficulties to give thanks.

Then let me remind you that the word *thank* is actually related to the word *think*. If you think it over, you have a lot to be thankful for. No matter what your situation, giving genuine, heartfelt thanks is always possible.

Matthew Henry, who lived from 1662 to 1714, was known for always being thankful. He always put words to his thankfulness, even the time he was robbed in the shadows of a dark street. He was bashed up against the wall and ordered to hand over all his money.

That night in his diary, Matthew wrote: "I am thankful that during all these years I have never been robbed until now. Also, even though they took my money, they did not take my life. And although they took all I had, it was not much. Finally, I am grateful that it was I who was robbed, not I who robbed."

On Day Three of the diet, you need to do two things. First, *practice the thousand thank-you's.*

Get by yourself, in a private room, outside in a park, or any place that feels right to you and then start saying, "Thank you." Say the words over and over again, a thousand times. That's right, a thousand times. Say it out loud or say it in your head, but make sure you say it.

Do this every third day on your diet, and you'll be amazed at the peace that washes over you. You'll be delighted by how much more positive you'll become.

Second, *express specific thanks.* Be on the lookout for things for which you can give thanks. It may be as simple as thanking someone who lets you go first in traffic, or it may be as silly as thanking a coworker who brightens your day with a joke. Thank as many people as you can on Day Three. You may even give your employer the same thing you expect—a little positive feedback. When all is said and done, new opportunities come to appreciative people more often than complaining people.

No matter what's going on in your life and in your world, you can always express some kind of specific thanks. I remember learning that lesson from Dr. Robert Schuller as he talked about the drought of the Great Depression. When harvest season came, his father normally gathered a hundred wagonloads of corn. But that year his father got a meager half wagonload.

Dr. Schuller says he'll never forget his dad's response. As they sat at the dinner table holding hands, his father said, "I thank you, God, that I have lost nothing. For I have regained the seed I planted in the springtime." He had planted a half wagonload of seed, and he harvested a half wagonload in the fall.

While other farmers were complaining about losing ninety to a hundred loads, Schuller's father taught him, "Never count up the might-have-beens or you'll be dejected. Never look at what you have lost. Look at what you have left." That's the way winners think and talk. And that's the way you will think and talk if you stay on plan for Day Three of your diet.

DAY FOUR: THINK POSITIVELY ABOUT YOURSELF

You've spent the first three days of your diet noticing the positive things going on around you. Now, on Day Four, you need to consciously, systematically think positively about yourself. This is not something you can leave to chance. You must work at it and make sure you do it.

First, *affirm yourself*. Affirmations were covered in a previous chapter and you should use them constantly, but on Day Four they need to be your primary focus.

Your affirmation can be as simple as "I love myself." Say it to yourself dozens of times throughout the day. It may be the most important thought you'll ever practice. And the more you say it, the more you'll feel it, believe it, and be it.

Second, *make an hourly list*. In other words, at the top of every hour, think of five good things about yourself.

You could remind yourself of the special knowledge, education, or ability that you have. You could recall some of your past victories. Or you could congratulate yourself on the good you have done and will do. The list of possibilities goes on and on.

Third, *refrain from making unhealthy jokes to put yourself down*. Don't say them, and don't even think them. There's nothing wrong with some good-natured playfulness or teasing. But negative people joke about their unhealthy behaviors rather than doing something about them. I've heard people say things like, "Seven days without pizza makes one weak." And, "One of life's greatest mysteries is how a two-pound box of candy can make you gain five pounds." I suppose that's why some say, "Brain cells come and brain cells go, but fat cells live forever."

If that's the way you take care of yourself, if that's the way you joke about yourself, then you can join the crowd that says, "Life not only begins at forty, it begins to show." Or, as my Great-Aunt Ella used to say, "I'm in shape. Round is a shape."

I know these comments are funny, but they aren't healthy. People who love themselves don't hurt themselves. They take care of themselves. Are you thinking positively about yourself? And are you taking care of yourself as a result? Or do you joke about how you abuse your health?

Fourth, *lighten up*. Don't take yourself too seriously on Day Four. Loosen up and laugh at yourself in a healthy way.

People who can't laugh at themselves are almost always negative thinkers, plagued with poor self-esteem. They have the hardest time with change, and as some physicians suggest, may be more susceptible to cancer, stroke, and heart disease.

So laugh. Lila Green, author of *Making Sense of Humor*, said, "When you laugh at yourself, you don't break—you bend."

The comedian George Burns exemplified that. At age ninety-three he signed a five-year contract with Caesar's Palace. When asked about it, he said, "They wanted me to sign a ten-year contract. That would be silly. How do I know they'll be around in ten years?"

Day Four is all about you. Spend the day thinking positive thoughts about yourself, and refuse to let any self-doubt enter your mind. Go for it!

DAY FIVE: SPEAK ONLY THE POSITIVE

Oftentimes, I've told my audience members that if they can't go twenty-four hours without an alcoholic beverage, they're addicted to alcohol. If they can't go twenty-four hours without a cigarette, they're addicted to nicotine. And if they can't go twenty-four hours without making a negative comment, they're addicted to negativity.

What about you? Can you go twenty-four hours without making one single negative comment? Most people can't.

Most people seem to be guilty of whining too much. Listen to them and you'll hear them say that you don't know the problems they have, that they can't do it, or that they tried one time and failed. They speak out verbal curses that kill off any attempts they might make at building a more positive attitude.

You need to discipline yourself to speak only the positive—at least one day every week. It may be the hardest thing you'll ever do, but it will eventually put you in control of your attitude.

First, *remove the word impossible from your vocabulary*. The most successful people avoid this word. They have removed the word from their vocabularies, and they refuse to say it. Some people even take out a pair of scissors and cut the word out of their dictionaries.

To become a more positive person, you've got to do the same thing. Refuse to use the word *impossible*. Don't say it, and don't write it. Don't even use similar phrases, such as "That will never work." They only create limitations and negativity.

Of course, this advice may sound silly, even outlandish. But positive people have learned to focus on what they can do instead of what they can't do. And positive people have learned that very few things in life are truly impossible. They tend to think that impossibility is nothing more than a big idea striking a small mind. Like Harry Emerson Fosdick said a hundred years ago, "The world is moving so fast these days that the person who says it can't be done is almost always interrupted by someone who is doing it."

Second, *hold back the negative utterances.* If you're not careful, if you live on autopilot, you may find yourself offering a steady negative commentary on the day. You may tell your coworker about the bad traffic on the way to work, and you may tell your spouse about the latest idiotic policy from Washington. If you let it, your negative commentary can go on and on.

So on Day Five, stop it! Don't say anything negative, and speak only the positive.

I know it will be difficult for you, and I know that cutting all the negative comments out of your conversations forever is unrealistic. Sometimes, you have to look at and talk about both sides of an issue. But for the purpose of practice, to take control of your attitude, refrain from all negative comments on this one day of the week.

You may have to talk yourself out of saying the negative things that come to mind. If, for instance, the man at the front of the company cafeteria line seems to be holding up everyone else, you might be tempted to make a snide remark to the person next to you. But don't do it. Stop yourself.

Ask yourself why you're making such a big deal out of a short delay. After all, there's still plenty of food left. And maybe you can force yourself to make a positive comment about the situation. Tell the person next to you, "It's kind of nice not to rush every single minute of the day."

Third, *verbalize the positive.* Go out of your way to talk optimistically about everything—your job, your customers, your manager, your children, your health, and your future. Look for something you like and comment on it. One person at work, for example, might have a great smile, and another one might be extremely dedicated to his work. So comment on these positive qualities.

Sally Jessy Raphaël showed her ability to verbalize the positive before she became a famous talk show host. In fact, in the first thirty years of her career, she was fired eighteen times. But every time it happened, she kept verbalizing the positive and set her sights on something better.

When no mainline U.S. radio station would hire her, mostly because she was a woman, she moved to Puerto Rico and polished her Spanish. When the wire service refused to send her to the Dominican Republic to cover an uprising, she scraped some money together, flew there on her own, and started to gather and sell her own news stories.

Finally, in 1982, she was asked to host a political radio talk show. She told her husband that she didn't know much about politics, so she would have to speak out of her heart.

She went on the radio, and drawing on her familiarity with a microphone and her easy confessional style, she talked about the Fourth of July and what it meant to her. She verbalized the positive. She invited callers to do the same, and she connected immediately with her listeners.

She became known as the Dear Abby of the airwaves and reached millions of viewers every day. And today, after all those struggles to succeed, she holds several Emmys.

What kind of reputation do you have? What do people say about you? Do they hear you verbalizing the positive on a regular basis? Or are they surprised when they hear a positive utterance come out of your mouth?

Remember, you can always find something positive to say. My daughter Rachel reminded me of that. Once, when she was seven, the two of us were playing the game *Candyland*. Unfortunately for her, she lost six games in a row. But every time she lost, she would clap her hands and cheer for me. She would say "Good job, Dad. You won! You won!"

Of course, I wished she had won a few games, but most of all I was confused by her response. Most kids don't cheer the opposition, and many have a hard time with losing. So I complimented her on being such a good sport. And I asked her, "How do you do that? You keep on losing but you keep on cheering for me. How do you do that?"

She said, "Dad, it's simple. I'm a positive thinker."

DAY SIX: DO POSITIVE THINGS FOR OTHERS

Even though society says it's okay to do whatever you want to do, and even though our culture advises you to look out for number one, that may not be the healthiest choice to make. Research has made it quite clear that the most positive people, the healthiest people, do positive things for others.

Allan Luk documents this idea in his book *The Healing Power of Doing Good*. In a carefully researched study of 3,300 people across the United States, 95 percent of those who helped others on a regular basis said they got a physical, emotional, and spiritual boost from the experience. Luk called it the "helper's high," and it came in two phases.

In phase one, an immediate sense of warmth, energy, and euphoria came over those who did positive things for others. In phase two, a calmer sense of well-being persisted long after the act of helping was completed.

So on Day Six of your diet, do positive things for others. It doesn't matter if you're too busy or too stressed out to even think about helping others. Luk and his subjects say helping isn't just a good way to relieve stress, it's the best way.

Lynn, for example, worked as the director of a private pre-school. She suffered from constant back pain that disappeared after she began volunteering at a local hospital. Tammy, a college student who struggled with horrific headaches, found that her headaches vanished whenever she volunteered. And Nat has survived seven years with the HIV virus by organizing AIDS fund-raisers and support groups. He says, "It's probably the only reason I'm alive today."

Helping others is obviously good for you and the people you're helping. It has an immediate and lasting impact on your overall health and attitude. But Luk says there is a proper way to do it if you're going to get all the benefits.

First, *there has to be some personal contact.* To release the healing power of doing positive things for others, you have to do more than send a check or drop off a bag of clothes at a mission. You have to spend time with the person you are helping. The warm emotions of the helper's high come out of the bonding that occurs with personal contact.

Second, *you have to spend about two hours a week helping.* Statistically speaking, Luk found that the helpers who spent two hours a week for ten weeks were the ones who felt the best and were the healthiest. Those who spent less than two hours helping had poorer health, and those who spent more than two hours did not receive any additional benefits.

Third, *you have to help strangers*. Those who only helped family and friends were the ones least likely to report the helper's high. After all, you're supposed to help them. By contrast, you help strangers because you want to. Helping strangers is a positive *choice*.

Michele Heisner made that choice in her quest to become a more positive person. She was a legal secretary in San Francisco, but she decided to offer her services at a community center in the city's tough Mission District. She signed up to be an English tutor.

The first night of her class Michele found herself in a room with three Mexican children. She spoke no Spanish, and they didn't speak any English. All they could do was point. Six months later, forty-seven children and adults were taking Ms. Heisner's course, laughing, learning, and sharing. And she got an immediate and lasting boost to her overall attitude.

As a young man, Richard Simmons also learned about the benefits of helping others. He had appeared in the early television Fruit of the Loom commercials. And even though he was a successful actor, he didn't feel good about himself because he had a weight problem. Then one day he found a note on his car that inspired him to do something about his problem. The note read, "Fat people die young. Please don't die."

Simmons went on a crash diet and lost 110 pounds in three months. Unfortunately, his dramatic weight loss damaged his body so severely that he had to be hospitalized. After this devastating experience, he decided to start all over and learn how to lose weight safely through sound nutrition and proper exercise. Once he learned that, he was determined to find some way to share his knowledge with others who were troubled with obesity.

He was so enthusiastic about his newfound knowledge, so excited about helping others, that people were immediately attracted to him. He made weight-loss education his business and enthusiasm his partner.

Today Richard Simmons is recognized across the world for his weight-loss crusade. But he couldn't have done it without first deciding to do something that would make a positive difference in the lives of others.

Throughout this book, I've given you dozens of strategies that will give you a more positive attitude. I hope you're using them, because they all work. But the neat thing about Day Six's program of doing positive things for others is that it not only gives you a more positive attitude, it also reduces your stress and increases your health—not to mention all the good it does for other people.

DAY SEVEN: TRY SOMETHING NEW

Monotony destroys optimism. As Dr. David Bouda said, "If you don't use your brain and body in different ways occasionally, then you will get old very quickly." So on Day Seven, try something new.

You get dozens of opportunities every day. Whether it's big or small, personal or professional, you can always try something new. Go to a museum. Sneak into a training session being given at your company. Walk through a new neighborhood. Check out a new shop. You'll be surprised by how these activities can lift your spirits.

The list of possibilities is endless. For example, have you dined at an entirely new ethnic restaurant in the last six months? Have you sought out information on the new, younger generation of workers and how to manage them? Have you personally purchased a new product or service via the Internet in the past thirty days? Do you own some new piece of electronic equipment and actually know how to use it? Have you rearranged the furniture in your office or living room in the past year? Have you changed your hair's style or color in the last eighteen months?

If you answered no to most of these questions, you may not be trying enough new things. You may need to follow Yogi Berra's advice: "When you come to a fork in the road, take it."

Of course, you may be saying, "So what! Why should I get in the habit of trying new things? What do I get out of it?" You get plenty. In fact, the benefits are enormous.

First, *you learn something.* When you try new things, you can't help but learn. Ralph Waldo Emerson put it this way, "All life is an experiment. The more experiments, the better." British philosopher Bertrand Russell believed, "In all affairs it's a healthy thing now and then to hang a question mark on the things you have long taken for granted."

You may be content with your learning from the past. You may be one of those people who seldom buy a nonfiction book to study, who seldom listen to CDs to master new areas of expertise, or who seldom attend a seminar that is not mandated by their employers.

If so, that's too bad. As 1990 Michigan Teacher of the Year Cynthia Ann Broad declared, "In times of change, it is the *learners* who will inherit the earth, while the *learned* will find themselves beautifully equipped for a world that no longer exists." You need to listen to the timeless advice of Mark Twain, "Take your mind out every now and then and dance on it. It is getting all caked up."

Second, *you have more fun.* Trying new things just makes life more enjoyable. Like the elderly man who was addressing his grandchildren, "Boys, I've never taken a drink, never eaten dessert, never ridden a motorcycle, never gone to bed after 10 p.m., and never even looked at a woman other than my wife. And you know what? Tomorrow I celebrate my hundredth birthday." After a pause, a voice from the back piped up and asked, "Celebrate? How?"

Are you having enough fun in life? Are you enjoying your work? Are you trying new things? Or are you stuck doing the same old things in the same old ways?

Of course, a new thing may not be fun the first time. Sometimes it takes a little practice to get the full enjoyment out of it. Think about it: Almost everything you do and do well, almost everything you enjoy, you practiced at some point in life. Like the American fellow who visited a London pub on a foggy night found, you can't judge too quickly. Hoping to strike up a conversation with a distinguished-looking Englishman, he asked, "May I buy you a drink?"

"No," said the Englishman. "Don't drink. Tried it once and I didn't like it."

Later the American fellow tried to make conversation again, and said, "Would you like a cigar?"

The Englishman said, "No. Don't smoke. Tried it once and I didn't like it."

The American thought for a moment. Then said, "Would you like to join me in a game of gin rummy?"

The Englishman replied, "No. Don't like card games. Tried it once, and I didn't like it. However, my son will be dropping in after a bit. Perhaps he will join you."

The American settled back in his chair and said, "Your only son, I presume?"

Third, *you'll probably live a longer, more positive life.* Margaret Rawson, an internationally recognized dyslexia researcher, demonstrated this when she took up flying at age seventy-two, learned to use a computer at eighty, and then published three books. In her nineties she said, "I have new projects ahead of me all the time. There's a lot I want to do and find out about, so I guess I'll just have to live another hundred years." She knows that trying new things keeps her young, positive, and energetic.

When I was a student years ago, one of my college professors told us about a study that examined the way living beings react to new things. Researchers placed four tubes on the floor, side by side, with a hunk of cheese placed in the second tube. They then released a mouse to see what he would do.

The mouse scurried through the first tube and discovered it was empty. He quickly went to the second tube, found the cheese, ate it, and went back to his cage.

The next day, the researchers did the same thing, and so did the mouse. It wasn't too long before the mouse was conditioned. He knew there was no cheese in the first tube, so he went directly to the second tube to get his reward.

After several days, the scientists moved the cheese from the second tube to the third one. The mouse was released, and, of course, he went directly to the second tube. It was empty.

So what did the mouse do? Did he go to the third tube, searching for the cheese? No. Did he go back to the first tube or on to the fourth one? No. He stayed in the second tube, waiting for the cheese to appear.

He had become accustomed to finding cheese in the second tube, and when that changed, he did not adjust. He did not explore any further. He wasn't willing to try anything new. If the scientists had allowed it, the poor mouse would have probably starved.

What about you? Are you starving to death in the second tube? Or are you trying new things? After all, you cannot discover new oceans unless you have the courage to lose sight of the shore.

On Day Seven, try some new things. You could change your morning routine. You could try getting up a half-hour earlier, eating out at a restaurant, taking a walk, or calling your mom. You could do a million new and different things, but do something. It will brighten your outlook.

Your Action Plan

After you've gotten through all seven days, start the whole process over again. Just keep on doing this, and you will not only have a positive attitude, you will release the power of a positive attitude into all parts of your life.

I don't know how long it will take for you to master the Seven-Day Mental Diet. I don't know how many negative attitudes you need to remove or how many positive attitudes you need to develop. But I do know that many people have accomplished more than ever before by taking this approach. Some people have mastered the diet in just one or two seven-day cycles. Other people have to consciously practice the cycle several times before it becomes instinctual.

It doesn't matter. Just do it until you've got it. And then you'll know what Wilfred Peterson was talking about in his book *The Art of Living* when he wrote that happiness is not what happens outside of you but what happens inside of you.

DISCIPLINE EXERCISES

One of the best ways to stay on a diet is to hold yourself accountable. Keep a record of what you are doing. Notice what works and doesn't work. Make adjustments as necessary. Do more of some things and less of others.

Make copies of this diet plan. Fill out a copy each week. And keep filling them out until you have mastered the diet and follow it almost automatically.

Day One: Feed your mind.

a. How did you feed your mind today?

b. What worked or didn't work? What do you need to do next time?

Day Two: See all the good around you.

a. What triggers have you established?

b. What good did you see today?

c. What changes do you need to make to ensure that you see all the good around you?

Day Three: Speak words of gratitude.

a. What words of thanks did you speak today?

b. What do you need to do differently to master this skill?

Day Four: Think positively about yourself.

a. How did you affirm yourself today? Were you able to laugh at yourself?

b. What new affirmations do you need to give yourself in the future?

Day Five: Speak only the positive.

a. How successful were you at holding back any negative utterances?

b. What positive comments did you make?

c. How could you be more effective in speaking only the positive?

Day Six: Do positive things for others.

a. What did you do for others today?

b. What kinds of things could you do for others in the future?

Day Seven: Try something new.

a. What did you do today that was new, different, or unique?

b. How did you gain from your new experience?

c. What kinds of new things could you do in the future that you would feel good about?

PART THREE

Staying On Course

CHAPTER EIGHT

Worry

STOP PAYING INTEREST ON A LOAN YOU NEVER HAD

If you really think about it, the only people who don't have problems are dead. Problems are a sign of life, and everyone is going to have problems every single day. But the good news is that you don't have to make things worse by worrying about them.

Unfortunately, most people choose to spend a great deal of time worrying. In fact, the average person probably spends more time worrying—about house payments, job complications, possible illnesses, or personal relationships—than thinking constructively. However, worry is a total waste. It will destroy your positive attitude, and it can destroy your life.

The Waste of Worry

Worrying wastes your life in four important ways.

1. WORRY WASTES YOUR TIME

In his book *Seeds of Greatness* Dr. Denis Waitley reported a study from the University of Michigan. The study discovered that most worries aren't "real." In fact, they found out that 95 percent of worries are unwarranted. They focus on something that happened in the past over which you have no control, or they focus on things that are simply petty. Only 5 percent of worries are real or justifiable. As Mark Twain once said, "I've had a long life. And I've had a lot of troubles. Most of which never happened."

Worrying wastes your time. For example, if you spend an hour a day worrying about something you have no control over, just think of all the time you lose. In a year, you will have worried for 365 hours. That's more than fifteen days of your life totally wasted! Just think of the difference it would make if you spent a fraction of that time doing something more productive and enjoyable, such as reading a self-help book or working on your attitude.

2. WORRY WASTES YOUR ENERGY

Remember the story of the children of Israel who left Egypt to go to the Promised Land? That journey should have taken eleven days, but it took them forty years. They were so worried they wouldn't be able to take over the Promised Land that they allowed it to slow them down. It wasn't distance that separated them from the Promised Land; it was worry.

In a very similar sense, worry wastes your energy. When you worry, your mind goes around and around in the same groove, and you never get anywhere. You don't come to any conclusions, and you don't solve any problems. So these behaviors are illogical and irrational, at best.

Strangely enough, worry usually makes things worse. The more you worry about something, the more upset you become. And the more upset you become, the more likely you are to make bad decisions, and bad decisions always lead to bad outcomes.

3. WORRY WASTES YOUR HEALTH

Medical studies show that worry is perhaps the most corrosive emotion to affect the body or mind. Dr. Alexis Carrel, the Nobel Prize winner in medicine, declared years ago that "Businessmen who do not know how to fight worry die young." And so do all professionals, construction workers, computer technicians, and everybody else.

The word *worry* comes from the Anglo-Saxon verb *rigan*. It means "choke" or "strangle." If someone were to come up to you, grasp you around the neck, and squeeze as hard as they could, they would be choking the life out of you. And you do the same thing to yourself when you spend time in useless worry.

Way back in the 1940s, Dr. O. F. Gober, chief physician of the Gulf, Colorado, and Santa Fe Hospital Association, said: "Seventy percent of all patients who come to physicians could cure themselves if they only got rid of their fears and worries." Ever since that time, doctors have been saying pretty much the same thing.

When you say, "I'm worried sick," many times that is exactly what happens. From a biological point of view, you are not constructed to handle the poisonous venom that worry injects into your system.

4. WORRY WASTES YOUR SPIRITUALITY

In its simplest terms, worry is negative goal setting. It focuses your attention on what you *don't* want to happen, which is the exact opposite of spirituality. Spirituality focuses your attention on what you *do* want to happen. The two fight against each other.

The plain truth is this: Worry and faith are incompatible. The more you have of one the less you have of the other. Even the Bible says that. In Philippians 4, verses 6 and 7, Paul says: "Don't worry about anything; instead pray about everything. Tell God what you need, and thank him for all he has done. If you do this, you will experience God's peace, which is far more wonderful than the human mind can understand." In other words, if you spend your time on worry, you won't experience peace.

Worry wastes your spirituality. A reporter found that out when he was given an exclusive interview with the devil. When the reporter arrived in hell, the devil gave him a tour through his hall of fame, where he displayed all the various weapons that he used to bring about war, crime, disease, and disaster. He carefully showed the reporter everything from cocaine to the nuclear bomb. Then the devil asked, "Would you like to see my favorite all-time most destructive weapon?" The reporter said, "You bet."

The devil became very excited. They walked down this long hall, deep into the dungeons of hell, and finally they arrived at a huge steel door locked closed by many heavy chains and bolts. The devil unlocked the door and swung it open. The reporter was surprised to see nothing but a little wedge of wood on an illuminated pedestal. The reporter asked, "What's this?"

"That," the devil explained, "is my greatest weapon of all time. It's the wedge of worry.

"Worry puts a wedge between you and God. And that's what I like to see—because then I've got you."

Where Does Worry Come From?

If worry is a total waste, you may be wondering why people bother to worry. Where does worry come from? Worry can come from a number of sources, but two causes in particular often give people the most difficulty.

One, *you may have been taught to worry about anything new, different, or out of the ordinary*. You may have been taught to equate the unknown with danger. I remember a television commercial that made this cause of worry very clear. The commercial featured an art teacher walking around a classroom saying, "The lines are our friends. Stay within the lines."

Perhaps you were told growing up to be careful, watch where you're going, take it easy, and not talk to strangers. Certainly some good existed in those messages, but you may have been preconditioned to be too cautious, and as a result, anything new may have become a cause for worry. And that worry of being "outside the lines" may have killed off some of your natural creativity.

You see this happen in lots of people. Up to the age of five, most kids use 95 percent of their creative capacity. Then they go to school, and by the age of twelve, they use only 20 percent of their creative capacity. By adulthood, the average person is down to 10 percent. Apparently the pressure to do the "right" thing, do what's expected, and maintain the "way we've always done it" gets so strong that it stifles creativity.

Two, *you may have been taught to strive for external security*. That's what most cultures teach, so it's no wonder if you bought into those beliefs.

Most secular cultures seem to say that you can be free of your worries and find true security if you just have enough of certain things. If you have enough money, a big enough house, a nice enough car, a good enough job, or a pretty enough spouse, then, they seem to say, you can be secure and have a life of joy and contentment.

When you think about it logically, this belief is ridiculous. You'll never have enough of anything to wipe away all your worries. A depression could come and wipe out all your money, your job, house, and cars. A huge conflict could destroy your relationships. Total external security is never possible. But if that's what you're working for, you'll always be prone to worry.

The only kind of security worth pursuing is internal security. With this type of security, you have so much confidence in yourself and so much faith in your God that you don't have room for worry.

What are you focused on—external or internal security? Here's a little test to find out.

Suppose you were abducted and dropped in a field somewhere in China. You have no Chinese language skills, money, or clothing; you're in a new culture and new climate. Would you survive or would you perish? Would you find a way to get shelter, make friends, and find food? Or would you freak out? If you had a great positive attitude, if you had internal security, you would do just fine.

By using the techniques in this chapter, you can get rid of your worries and gain internal security.

Worry Is a Choice

You may be thinking, "I've spent my whole life worrying. There's nothing I can do about it. That's just the way I am. I can't help it." But you do have a choice; you can choose to let go of worry.

But lots of people don't want to let go. They act like a certain group of monkeys in Africa does. A group of scientists knew that this particular kind of monkey could be captured for study if they simply gave the monkeys the right kind of choice. So the scientists went out in the jungle and made a trap out of a glass bottle with a long, narrow neck. They filled the bottle with nuts, staked it to the floor of the jungle, and went back to camp, confident that the monkeys would be easily captured.

And indeed they were. The monkeys smelled the nuts, put their hands in the bottle, and grabbed a fistful. And then they were trapped. Their fists would no longer fit through the narrow neck of the bottle because they wouldn't let go of the nuts.

You might smile and think, "How silly." And yet, you may be guilty of behaving the same way. Your problems may stick to you because you simply won't let go. You choose to keep on worrying about them. But you can choose to replace your worries with healthier behavior. Stop the worrying and get a better attitude by using the following nine techniques.

1. PUT WORRY INTO PERSPECTIVE

All too often, people jump to conclusions without getting the whole picture. And all too often, they jump to horrifying conclusions that bring on needless worry.

Do you ever do that? Or do you wait until you get all the facts before reacting one way or another? As I would tell my students years ago, "Withhold evaluation until comprehension is complete."

One mother was guilty of jumping to conclusions. As she prepared dinner in the kitchen, her little boy and the neighbor girl played in the sandbox outside. Suddenly through the kitchen window she heard the little boy say, "That's not the way my mother makes love." The mother was horrified and ran outside to investigate what was going on. She found her little son in a superior manner looking down at the girl who had etched the letters L-U-V in the sand with her finger. Seeing the whole story, her worries dissipated.

When you're about to worry, you also need to get the whole story. Put things in perspective. You'll find that your worries may seem rather trifling, or they may even go away.

I learned that many years ago, when I visited the refugee camps in Thailand back in the 1980s. During that time, hundreds of thousands of people were fleeing to the safety of Thailand from the genocide taking place in Laos and Cambodia.

But they couldn't stay there forever. So the frightened refugee families were interviewed by interpreters, United Nations officials, and placement specialists. I sat in those interviews and listened to the questions. Where might the families go? Everyone had a desire to go home, but if going home meant an almost certain death, where could the refugee families be sent? It was a worrisome question, to be sure.

And then it hit me. I was worried about the flies in the refugee camp. I was worried about how nice my hotel room would be that night, and I was worried about the quality of the meal I would be served. When I put my worries into perspective, when I gave the refugee families a bit more empathy, all of my worries seemed to be somewhat irrelevant—or at least miniscule by comparison.

The next time you're about to worry, gain some perspective by thinking about the worries you had five years ago. Chances are you can't even remember them, because they really weren't a big deal. Of the ones you do remember, how many actually came to pass? Probably not very many. So ask yourself when you feel overcome with worry, how important will this be in five years?

2. REALIZE YOU CAN COPE

Regardless of what you might tell yourself, you're not weak and you're not incompetent. You probably have a great deal more power than you realize. And you have more than enough energy to handle almost any situation that comes your way. So don't sell yourself short. Realize that you can cope, and you have no need to worry.

One of my students, Paul, showed me what can happen when you finally realize you can cope. You don't have to worry, and you can move on with your life.

When Paul was born, he was badly deformed. His arms and legs were so twisted that he never learned to walk or care for himself. At age eight, Paul heard the doctors tell his parents that he wouldn't live that long, so there was no sense in "wasting" any time or money on him. His parents were told it would be best to put him in an institution.

So that's where Paul lived—until he was sixty-eight. It was then that Paul decided he had had enough. He was tired of worrying about his future. He wanted to live, not just exist. So he planned out his life and decided to go for it.

That's when I met Paul. He showed up in one of my classes at the university where I taught. Paul said he wanted to get a college degree, then a master's degree, and go into the counseling profession. He wanted to help other people.

I couldn't help but admire him. Paul had so little. He had hardly any money, no family members, and only a few years of life. All he had was the person he hired to push him from class to class, care for his physical needs, and write out the papers he dictated. But he had a plan, and he was taking the risks to make his plan a reality.

I watched Paul move ahead as he took several classes from me at the university. I watched him as he started a toastmasters' club on campus and as he got elected to a seat on the student senate. Paul had learned that he could cope with his challenges.

Can the same be said about you? Do you feel up to the task and up to the challenge? Or do you doubt yourself and worry about whether or not you can handle the situations in front of you? If you doubt yourself and need a bit more confidence, spend some more time with the chapter on self-esteem. You simply should not minimize what you are able to do and what you're able to cope with.

Kemmons Wilson, the founder of Holiday Inn, realized he could cope. In fact, it was the very skill that made him successful. When he was asked to speak at his former high school, Kemmons said, "I do not know why I'm here. I didn't graduate from high school, and I never worked a full day in my life. So I'll give you the advice I follow. Just work half days, and it doesn't matter which twelve hours you work, the first half or the second half."

3. DO IT ANYWAY

Perhaps the wisest American to have ever lived was Ralph Waldo Emerson. He said, "Do the thing you fear and the death of fear is certain." In other words, it takes action to get rid of a worry. Instead of thinking about your worrisome situation over and over, take action and the worry will go away.

Let's say, for example, that you're worried about an upcoming conversation you need to have with your boss. You spend days and nights worried about what you should say. In fact, you get so worried that you don't say anything at all, you just stew over it.

A person with a positive attitude would do it anyway. She would think about what needed to be said and the best way to say it. And then she would go ahead and say it. No matter what the outcome, that particular worry would be gone.

Robert Louis Stevenson, the author of *Treasure Island*, knew about the strategy of doing it anyway. In his spare time he canoed, sailed, hiked, and traveled. But it wasn't widely known that Stevenson suffered from years of illness. He talked in his books of going to bed weary and getting up sick, year after year. He finally died of tuberculosis and a stroke at age forty-four.

Now, he could have lived his whole life filled with worry. He could have worried about his health and what would become of him. He could have worried his life away and done nothing. But he did it anyway. Stevenson wrote, "I was made for a contest. And the powers that be have willed that my battlefield shall be the inglorious one of the bed and the medicine bottle." I beg to differ. A person who stands up to worry, fear, and pain is not inglorious. He's a champion.

Maurice Chevalier showed us that. Even though he was one of the most famous actors of his time, in the middle of his career he suffered a setback. As he was going on stage one night, he felt terribly dizzy. His brain seemed on fire, and the cues reached him from a far distance. He stammered, he stumbled, and the other actors had to cover for him that night. They covered for him for weeks and weeks, and finally he couldn't go on any longer. He needed the care of a doctor.

Chevalier was filled with worry about his health, his acting career, and his future. He was worried that it might all be over. So his doctor told him to spend a few weeks in a small town in the southern part of France, take some long walks, and repair his damaged nervous system. Eventually the doctor told him, "There's a small village hall in that little town. I want you to give a performance to the people."

Chevalier answered, "I can't. I'm terrified. What guarantee is there that my mind won't go blank again?"

The doctor said, "There are no guarantees. But fear is never a reason for quitting. It is only an excuse." In other words, do it anyway.

Chevalier did perform in that small village hall, and it went fairly well. And he used that strategy for the rest of his career. He experienced many moments of fear and worry, but he never let it stop him again. He simply admitted the fear and did it anyway.

Later on in life, Chevalier made a comment that is good advice for all of us. He said, "If you wait for the perfect moment, when all is safe and all is assured, it may never arrive. Mountains will not be climbed, races won, or lasting happiness achieved." So go ahead and do it anyway.

In each of these cases, you'll notice a similarity. Emerson, Stevenson, and Chevalier weren't playing mental games. They didn't deny the challenges and struggles in front of them. They honestly admitted their fears and worries, but they refused to let worry take over. They took action instead. And their worries lost all power over them.

The same thing will happen for you if you follow this approach. Stand up to your worry. Do it anyway.

4. FORGET YOURSELF

One of the great psychiatrists of the twentieth century, Dr. Karl Menninger, was addressing a large audience of psychologists and psychiatrists on the topic of mental health. A question-and-answer period followed his speech. One person asked, "Dr. Menninger, if you were to meet somebody about to have a nervous breakdown, what would you advise the person to do?" Everyone expected him to recommend professional help. But Dr. Menninger, the old wise man, the great guru, said, "I'd tell them to go out and help somebody, because they almost always get healthy."

Worry is self-absorption. It puts an extreme emphasis on self. What should *I* say? What should *I* do? What will others think of *me*? It's all about *me, me, me*. But as Menninger knew, if you stop thinking about yourself, at least temporarily, if you think about others and how you can help them, your worries will go away. You'll get healthy and have a more positive attitude.

Florence Nightingale, the founder of the modern nursing profession, changed the whole world when she learned this strategy. When she stopped thinking about herself and thought about others, her worries died and her success grew.

At one point she wrote in her diary, "My God, what will become of me. I have no desire but to die. There is not a night that I do not lie down in my bed wishing that I may live no more. Unconsciousness is all that I desire." Talk about worry and despair!

When she died sixty years later, it was said that she, along with the inventor of chloroform and the inventor of antiseptic, was one of the three people who alleviated the most suffering in the nineteenth century.

And how did she get beyond her worries? She forgot about herself temporarily, and went out and helped somebody else. I don't see any reason why you can't go out and do likewise.

5. PRACTICE THE PRESENCE OF GOD

As mentioned above, worry and faith are incompatible. Worry and faith sit on opposite ends of the same teeter-totter. As your faith goes up, worry goes down. That's why someone wrote long ago, "Fear knocked at the door. When faith answered, no one was there."

Of course, words like *faith*, *God*, and *spirituality* may seem like rather inappropriate words for a secular book on positive attitudes. And I know they are controversial, if not politically incorrect, topics for lots of people. I'm not here to preach or tell you what to believe. But I do feel responsible for telling you what works, and faith in God has worked for millions of people over the centuries. Faith is a very effective way of destroying negativity and worries and building positive attitudes.

So how do you get more faith? One simple thing you can do is to practice the presence of God. Just imagine that God, the source of all that is good and positive, is right there with you. Think about it. Picture it. Visualize his presence. The more you practice, the less you worry.

Brother Lawrence learned the power of this technique hundreds of years ago. A simple man who worked his entire adult life in the kitchen of a French monastery, he never liked his work. The hours were long and the work was hard, but he found a way to live a very happy, rewarding, and rich life by practicing the presence of God. He said it turned away his worries and frustrations as it brought about peace and tranquility.

Whenever Brother Lawrence worked in the kitchen he would think, "God is here, right now, with me." He would pray that God would be with him and give him peace. And those moments became very special to him. Some years later he wrote in his book, *Practice the Presence of God*, "I would rather pray in my kitchen among the noise and clatter of the pots and pans than go to the most beautiful cathedral and commune there."

If practicing the presence is difficult or seems too esoteric for you, you might try what Earl Hipp, the president of Human Resource Development, Inc., recommends. He suggests that you picture yourself on a bicycle, traveling through your day, with God at the helm. He calls it "God on a Bike."

> At first I saw God as my observer, my judge, keeping track of the things I did wrong, so as to know whether I merited heaven or hell when I die. He was out there sort of like the president. I recognized his picture when I saw it, but I didn't really know him.
>
> Later on when I began to recognize my Higher Power, it seemed as though life was rather like a bike ride, but it was a tandem bike, and God was in the back helping me pedal.

I don't know just when it was that he suggested that we change places, but life has not been the same since. Life with my Higher Power, that is. Life has gotten more exciting with God on the front seat.

When I had control, I knew the way. It was a lot of work and often rather boring and predictable. It was usually the logically, shortest distance between any two points.

But when God took the lead, he knew delightful long cuts, up mountains, and through rocky places at breakneck speeds. It was all I could do to hang on! Even though our journey looked like madness, he said, Pedal.

I worried and was anxious and asked, "Where are you taking me?" He laughed and didn't answer. That is when I started to learn to trust him.

I forgot my boring life and entered into the adventure. And when I'd say, "I'm scared," he would lean back and touch my hand.

He took me to people with gifts that I needed, gifts of healing, acceptance, and joy. They gave me their gifts to take on my journey, our journey, God's and mine.

Then we would be off again. He said, "Give the gifts away; they're extra baggage, too much weight." So I did, to all the people we met, and I found that in giving I received, and still our burden was light.

I did not trust him at first, in control of my life. I thought he'd wreck it. But he knows bike secrets, knows how to make it bend to take sharp corners, jump to clear high rocks, and fly through short and scary passages.

Now I'm learning to shut up and pedal in the strangest places. I'm beginning to enjoy the view and the cool breeze on my face. And when I forget, become fearful and feel as if I just can't do it anymore, I feel God smiling and hear the gentle voice that says, "You just pedal."

Need a bit more peace? A little less worry? Practice the presence of God. Take two or three minutes each day to actually visualize something like Brother Lawrence recommends—or even something as whimsical as God on a bike. I know it works for me.

If you're struggling with this concept, you might remember the eighty-year-old couple driving down the highway. As they were driving, Ma turned to Pa and asked, "Pa, whatever happened to us? Remember how it used to be years ago, when we first got married? I'd sit close to you in the car, lay my head on your shoulder, look in your eyes, and tap your knee. And now look at us. You're over there; I'm over here. Whatever happened to us, Pa?"

He replied, "Ma, I ain't moved!"

The same thing applies to our spiritual lives. As the old line goes, "If you feel distant from God, guess who moved?" It's worth remembering if you're trying to overcome your worries and maintain your positive attitude.

6. STAY IN THE PRESENT

If you live your life in the future or in the past, you are going to have problems with worry, because that's where worry lives. Worry has a difficult time living in the present.

Perhaps you're worried about the future. Some people are constantly tied up in knots, worried about what tomorrow might bring. These people live their lives in the future. I remember when my brother and I were little we would ride in the back seat of our car, with my mom and dad in the front. We'd ask the normal childhood questions, "How long is it going to take? When are we going to be there?" My mom, the great worrier, would turn to us and reply, "How do we even know *if* we are going to get there?" She was worried about the future.

Other people worry about the past. They think about the pain, the guilt, and the bad things that have happened to them. My grandmother was that way. Give her a chance and she would tell you what somebody said to her seventy-five years ago. She would say such things as, "Back in 1922, Elsie said blah-blah-blah. And do you know what? She never apologized!" My grandmother, as dear as she was, never learned the wisdom of Confucius, who said, "To be wronged is nothing, unless you continue to remember it."

The sad thing about living in the future or the past is that you could live your whole life and completely miss everything. But if you learn to live in the moment, right in the present, you'll get rid of the worries.

I had to learn this skill. I used to spend much of my life living in the future and the past. Even when I took vacations, I would be worried about the work I had to do when I got back home, or I would be worried about something I should have done before I left home. I was supposedly on vacation, but I wasn't "there" when I was there.

It's taken me a few years, but I've learned something about staying in the present. I've learned, for example, that when I'm hiking in the mountains, focusing on the beauty around me is more invigorating than worrying about how long it will take to get to the end of the trail. And I've learned that when it comes to work, focusing on the most important task on my desk is less worrisome than thinking about all the other things I have to do in the next few days. When I'm totally absorbed in the present, I cannot worry.

This skill is not easy to learn, but you can do it. Start to be aware of those times when your mind wanders off to the future or the past. You may find yourself, for example, thinking about tomorrow's sales presentation while your spouse is talking to you. When you catch yourself doing it, stop! Bring your mind back to what your spouse is saying or whatever else is happening right in front of you. With practice you can discipline your mind to stay focused on the present.

7. USE YOUR IRA ACCOUNT

A psychiatrist once told me that the chief duty of a human being is to endure life. I thought about it and realized that if the purpose of life is just to be endured, how pathetic and miserable existence really is. Yes, we're going to have problems, but there's more to life than just enduring it.

Vice President Hubert Humphrey, even when he was dying, had a much more optimistic outlook. He said the chief duty of a human being is to enjoy life. And one way to enjoy life is to use your IRA account.

In the financial world, an IRA refers to a person's saved-up money and resources. But in the sometimes crazy, emotional world of worry, IRA refers to *inspect*, *respect*, and *act*. It refers to a logical three-step sequence that you can and should apply to your worries.

First, inspect the worry. In fact, you might even sit down and inspect all your worries. Take them apart ruthlessly. Designate an entire hour each month as your worry day. Put a great big red *W* on your calendar, and take a few minutes to write down all your worries and fears. Then go through each worry and ask yourself, what is the worst thing that could happen in that situation? You might find that even if that particular worry becomes reality, it is not that big a deal.

Then ask yourself, how likely is that worst thing to occur? You'll probably find that most of your worries aren't very likely to happen; they have very little substance. They're not worth worrying about.

Back in 1953, Walt Disney applied this first step, the inspect step, at a big convention in Chicago. All the amusement park owners in the United States were gathered together at a late-night session, and Disney talked to them about his plan for a new kind of amusement park. They all said he was crazy and that the special effects he had in the movies could not be pulled off in an amusement park. They were all worried about impending failure. Disney inspected their worries as well as his own. He concluded that the worries were not worth heeding, and said, "I know better than to kill an idea without giving it a chance to live."

Of course, at times a worry of yours will seem somewhat reasonable. That's when you apply the second step. You respect that particular worry.

You may find, for example, when you're going through the inspect step and you ask yourself what the worst thing that could happen is, that that worst thing probably will happen. Your worry is not groundless. Your worry cannot and should not be ignored. So respect it. Pay attention to it and decide to do something about that particular worry.

At this point, the third step of your IRA kicks in immediately. You act. You may call someone you admire or someone who has gone through a similar problem. You may get some advice on what to do. And then you do something that prevents your worry from coming to fruition, or at least takes the sting out of it.

So inspect, respect, and act. It works. Murphy proved that. Back in the 1920s, Murphy was a successful agent on Broadway booking dog acts and jugglers. You may remember the so-called Murphy's Law. He said, "If anything can go wrong it will go wrong." That makes him sound terribly negative, as if he was a man filled with worry. But that was just the beginning of what he said. Murphy went on, "Therefore you anticipate it, you prepare for it, and then you need no excuses." You inspect, respect, and act.

8. USE SELF-ENCOURAGEMENT

Many people add to their worries by asking what-if questions, such as, "What if the car breaks down?" or "What if I lose my job?" But asking these types of questions and filling your head with negative thoughts can be extremely destructive.

A New York physician confirmed the destructiveness of negative thoughts when one of her patients, a local businessman, had a nervous breakdown. The patient said, "I'm sure it's just from working too much."

The doctor replied, "People seldom have nervous breakdowns from overwork. Primarily, they think themselves into them." Nervous breakdowns happen when people give themselves too many negative, worrisome messages.

Instead of worrying, you should fill your head with self-encouragement. For example, maybe you are afraid of trying new things. Rather than avoiding everything new, you could tell yourself, "If I don't do it now I'll just have to do it later." Or maybe you are afraid of being honest with someone about your feelings. Rather than worrying about the other person's reaction, you could tell yourself, "If I don't tell her how I feel, she'll never know what I need." Self-encouragement will make it easier for you to confront your worries.

I learned that lesson as a young man. Back in high school, I was under the impression that great grades led to great scholarships at great universities. So I studied all the time and graduated at the top of my class. But the scholarships didn't come.

Due to financial necessity, I was more or less forced to live at home and attend the local college in town. And I wasn't happy about it. My dream of going to a prestigious private university far away had been dashed. Life felt unfair, and I spent my freshman year feeling angry and depressed.

Then in April of my freshman year, I saw an ad in the college newspaper for exiting, high-paying summer jobs in Europe. I thought that was for me. It would be an escape from my gloomy outlook on life.

Two months later I arrived in London, eager to earn the big money and experience great adventure. It was then that I met a kindly old gentleman, quite by accident, and we discussed my upcoming job. He looked at my papers and said, "Oh, nobody has told you, have they? We get a lot of young American kids here in the summertime. We call those jobs 'slave labor.'"

I did some quick checking. I found out that my job was bussing tables in a restaurant, seven days a week, twelve hours a day, and that the pay was $14 a week. Now I was more upset than ever. I quickly telegraphed my father and asked him what I should do. He sent back a one-sentence response that read, "You can take anything for a short period of time."

He was right. I took the job. I worked very hard those summer months. But I look back and realize that that was one of the most maturing experiences in my life. I learned that I *could* take anything for a short period of time. And I have used the same skill of self-encouragement thousands of times over the years. It has helped me confront and overcome my worries.

What about you? Are you asking yourself too many worrisome what-if questions? Or are you encouraging yourself?

In one of my seminars, a participant spoke out and said he had always wanted to go to law school, but he allowed his negative worries to stop him. What if he couldn't get into law school? What if he couldn't pass the bar exam? "Besides that," he said, "I'm thirty-six. It would take three years to finish, and by then I'd be *thirty-nine.*"

One of his coworkers in the seminar responded, "You can be thirty-nine and a lawyer, or you can just be plain thirty-nine. It's your choice."

It was exactly what the man needed to hear. It changed his life. He began telling himself, "I'm a thirty-nine-year-old lawyer," using the sentence as the bit of self-encouragement that got him into law school and through his bar exam.

I encourage you to write up some similar sentences. Have some encouraging phrases at your disposal and ready for use when worry comes into your life.

If you just can't think of anything encouraging to tell yourself, if you're so far down and so deeply stuck in your worries, use the "cancel-cancel" technique. When a worry comes along, firmly and forcefully tell yourself to "cancel-cancel." The worry will stop. It will be moved from the center stage of your mind.

Of course, your worry might come back, and it might come back rather quickly. It may be your habitual way of thinking. No problem. Just keep on telling your mind to "cancel-cancel" when the worry comes, and it will eventually be eliminated.

So what encouragement are you going to give yourself? The time to figure it out is now.

9. LEARN THE ART OF SAUNTERING

Henry David Thoreau, the author of *Walden*, said, "It's a great art to saunter." In other words, slowing down your life has great value. It helps to remove the worry.

Of course, in today's world, slowing down seems to be an almost foreign concept, like little Jeremy pointed out when he was getting ready for bed one night. His father still wasn't home from work, and the boy was scared. He asked, "Mommy, why isn't Daddy here?" She explained that Daddy hadn't finished his work at the office today, so he couldn't come home. He said, "Mommy, why don't they put him in a slower group?"

Not a bad question, because nothing affects the quality of life more than the pace of it. Many people rush to get up in the morning, rush to work, rush to finish their work, and then rush back home. They never take time to get in tune with themselves and the people around them. And worries thrive at this rushed pace.

By contrast, *sauntering* means moving at a leisurely pace. One of the simple ways to slow down and saunter is to take a walk. The rhythms of your body, mind, and spirit get in tune with each other when you walk. You'll begin to notice more and more of the things around you, you'll feel more at peace, and your worries will seem less significant.

Thoreau struggled for a long time with worry until he learned the art of sauntering. It was so therapeutic that he went on to plead with people and tell them to "live in each season as it passes. Breathe the air."

How are you doing in that department? Are you living life now, or merely rushing through it?

Goodbye Worry! Hello Positive Attitude!

It would not be too much of an exaggeration to say that attitude is everything. In fact, your attitude toward something is often a great deal more important than the event itself. That's why the English poet John Milton wrote over 300 years ago:

> The mind is its own place, and in itself
> Can make a heaven of Hell, a hell of Heaven.

And nothing does more to destroy your positive attitude than worry. Napoleon and Helen Keller made that clear. Both had plenty to worry about, but one conquered it and the other didn't. Napoleon had everything—fame, power, and wealth—and yet he said, "I have never known six happy days in my life." Helen Keller, on the other hand—who was blind, deaf, and mute—declared, "I have found life so beautiful." The difference was all in the way they handled their worries.

Use some of the nine techniques outlined above to remove your worries. As you remove your worries, you make room for your positive attitudes to grow.

WORRY EXERCISES

One of the most destructive, negative feelings is worry. Worry is the number-one block to risk and change. It also serves as a major obstacle to success, happiness, and achievement in life.

1. Evaluate Your Anxiety Level

Indicate how much anxiety you have in each of the following situations. Use the following scale:

M = Much
S = Some
L = Little

If your answer is *Much*, write a sentence that explains why that situation worries you.

Example: If in response to "r", "Making mistakes," you wrote "Much," you might then write, "I am afraid that people will think I'm stupid."

a. Someone speaking to me loudly

b. Speaking in public

c. Being around crazy people

d. Being teased

e. Failing at some task

f. Being with strangers

g. Feeling angry

h. Being with people in authority

i. Having feelings of tenderness and love

j. Expressing feelings of tenderness and love

k. Being watched while at work

l. Receiving a compliment

m. Being criticized

n. Having someone express anger to me

o. Being ignored

p. Looking foolish

q. Being disliked

r. Making mistakes

s. Having a lull in the conversation

2. Tackle Your Worries

a. Discuss some of the things you were worrying about last year at this time. Were the worries real or imagined?

b. What are your top five worries today?

c. How is worry holding you back? For example, how is the fear of going for the big sale, promoting new ideas, or communicating your feelings getting in your way?

d. Write out a plan of action for attacking each of your worries from above. Refer to and use some of the techniques discussed in this chapter.

CHAPTER NINE

Failure

FAILURE IS NOT FALLING DOWN, BUT STAYING DOWN

It Ain't Over Until You Win

Successful people—people with positive attitudes—accept failure as an inevitable part of the process that leads to success.

Motivational speaker Les Brown illustrates the point when he talks about a time when his son was eleven years old. The two of them were playing a board game, and for ten games straight Les won every one of them. Finally, Les said, "Son, it's getting late. Time for bed."

The boy pleaded, "Aw, Dad. Just one more game." But Dad kept insisting it was time for bed.

Lightning struck when his son countered, "Dad, you don't understand! It ain't over until I win!" Now that's good advice for all of us. It ain't over until you win.

Disrespect for Failure

Unfortunately, our culture has a deep disrespect for failures, mistakes, and setbacks. I saw a sign on one boss's desk that read, "Do you like to travel? Do you like to meet new friends? Would you like to free up your future? All this can be yours if you make just one more mistake!"

At another company, I saw a sign that read, "Failure: The line of least resistance." That statement could be true in some cases. Some people fail because they're just plain lazy. But lumping all failures into that category is a mistake.

The truth is quite different. If you interview truly successful individuals, you'll soon learn that none of them achieved success overnight. Their recognized successes came after lots of work and lots of setbacks. In fact, it was their failures—and their attitude towards those failures—that taught them how to do it better the next time around.

Struggles Will Come

Constant effort and frequent mistakes have almost always preceded phenomenal success. As the great opera singer Beverly Sills said, "There are no shortcuts to anyplace worth going."

Sometimes mistakes and failures just happen. Even though your intentions are good and your efforts are strong, some things just don't turn out the way you would like them to.

You've got to accept the fact that you will struggle as you work on yourself and your goals. But struggle can be good if you handle it appropriately. It can build your attitude as it builds your character, and character leads to success.

Truly happy, successful people know that hard work will pay off later while laziness pays off now. That was certainly the case for Steve Allen, the star and original host of the "Tonight!" show, which popularized late-night talk shows and continued successfully ever after. He overcame exceptional hardships in childhood before reaping the rewards of success later in life.

He was born in New York City in 1921, the child of an abusive mother who frequently vented her vicious temper on him. To make things worse, Steve was often left with a variety of alcoholic aunts and uncles so his vaudeville parents could go on tour.

At age thirteen, Steve ran away from home to seek refuge with an aunt in California, riding his bicycle most of the way across the United States until it broke. He continued his journey on freight trains, eating ant-covered leftovers that wandering drifters had left behind.

Interestingly enough, Steve Allen never gave up the struggle, even when he "had it made" and didn't have to work anymore. He dedicated the last few years of his life to the Parents Television Council, a national effort to clean up the filth that permeates so much of today's television programming.

Losers tend to be very envious of successful people like Steve Allen. All they see is the end result. They don't see the struggle and the failure along the way. They don't see the indomitable positive attitude that kept him going. They say, "I could have done that if I'd been in his shoes. He had all the right breaks. I could be successful too, if times weren't so tough, if I could just get some breaks in life."

The truth is that successful people wouldn't be the successes they are without all the struggles they have had. Successful people accept the struggle as part of the process. Just like Steve Allen, they make a conscious decision to keep on keeping on until they succeed.

A Healthy Definition of Failure

Regardless of who you are or what you're trying to accomplish, you're going to have some struggles and failures as you try to achieve more and more. And that's no big deal. You shouldn't expect anything else. Champions know that the process of becoming a champion is hard.

But they also know that champions do not become champions in the ring. They are merely recognized in the ring—because they have a healthy definition of failure. They say that failure is not the falling down, but the staying down. And the two are very different.

After all, no one succeeds all the time. People with a positive attitude accept that. They accept failure as a natural part of life, so they don't get bent out of shape when failure comes. They see failure as a mere stop on the road, while losers see failure as the end of the road.

Perhaps no one knew that better than singer and actress Debbie Reynolds. When she was a young girl in Texas, Debbie and her family were forced to live with her grandparents during the Depression because her father could not find work. Food was scarce, and space was limited. They survived by eating jackrabbit, and people slept four to a bed.

Looking for better times, Debbie's family moved to California. At age sixteen Debbie won the Miss Burbank contest, which led to an acting part in a movie. Marriage followed, but that ended in a bitter divorce, leaving her to raise two children alone.

Her second marriage was to a millionaire shoe manufacturer, but that ended when his financial gambles caused the failure of his business. He took off, leaving Debbie with millions of dollars of debt. The banks repossessed everything, including her home.

Determined to pay off the debts and properly care for her family, she went on the road doing live theater. It took her over ten years to pay off the debt her ex-husband left her, but she did it.

Of course, over the years, Debbie Reynolds has had numerous successes. But she's also faced a long string of problems. She just refused to quit.

Debbie says her secret is simple: She gets up after she falls down. She knows that failure is not the falling down but the staying down. She knows that success is getting up just one more time than you fall down.

The nineteenth-century English poet William Blake expressed the same sentiment. He wrote, "Mistakes are easy, mistakes are inevitable, but there is no mistake so great as the mistake of not going on."

Of course, you would probably like to avoid all mistakes and failures in life. You would probably like to have instant success. Who wouldn't? Well, that's not going to happen. So you need to know how to maintain your positive attitude and deal with failure when it comes your way. You need to know how to get up just one more time. The following strategies will help you do that.

1. REFUSE TO BLAME ANYONE OR ANYTHING FOR YOUR FAILURES

Dr. William Glasser, the author of *Reality Therapy*, has found two types of people in the world. Some people are happy and healthy, and they truly enjoy life. Other people are unhappy and unhealthy, and they're disgruntled with life.

The difference between these two types is perspective. Happy people spend time in self-evaluation, which leads to self-improvement and a high quality of life. They take responsibility. They focus on what they can do to make things better when they fall down.

By contrast, unhappy people evaluate everything and everyone except themselves. They blame other people and circumstances for their difficulties. Their mistakes are always someone else's fault. They focus on what others did that "caused" their failure.

Obviously, you want to be solidly placed in the first group. So do I. The truth is, though, that very few people are. According to Lewis Timberlake, in his book *It's Always Too Soon to Quit*, statistics show that only 10 percent actually succeed at their goals and make the improvements to themselves that build a quality life. Another 10 percent are at the other extreme, so unhappy with their defeats and difficulties that they turn to desperate measures, such as drugs, alcohol, illicit sex, and suicide.

Most people—80 percent—live somewhere between these two extremes. They simply endure life. They have dreams, but they're convinced they'll never be achieved. They have jobs they don't like, but they don't do anything about it. They're frustrated because they didn't get the right breaks in life.

In reality, people don't fail because they don't get the right breaks. People fail because they don't think the thoughts and take the actions that will change their circumstances. And people stay stuck in their failures when they blame anyone or anything for their failures. Blame immobilizes.

Take your job, for example. You may feel like a failure. You may feel stuck in a job that is going nowhere, or you may think your company does nothing to invest in your career development. You could spend hours in the employee lounge talking about those issues, but as long as you blame the boss or the company, you'll never do anything about your failure.

Or maybe you feel slighted when it comes to education. You never had the chance to get the schooling you wanted. As someone once said, "When I went to school, all I had was a pencil and the kid next to me. And I think if he'd really applied himself, I could have been somebody."

Like the father who asked his fighting sons, "What's going on here?" One son said, "Well, Dad, it all started when Tommy hit me back." No responsibility, just blame.

So I suggest three things. First, stop blaming. Of course, that's easier said than done. Blaming another person or factor is a natural reaction to failure. After all, your company, boss, parents, friends, or spouse might deserve some blame. They might have contributed to your failure.

For instance, there's the story about a set of identical twins who were raised by an almost constantly drunk father. At age fourteen the twins were sent to separate foster homes, not to be reunited for some thirty years.

When they were brought together at age forty-four, they were interviewed on a TV talk show. One of the twins had become an alcoholic like his father, while the other one had become an anti-alcohol advocate.

When the TV host asked them why they turned out the way they did, they both gave the same answer. Each of them said, "What do you expect? How could I turn out any differently considering the father I had?"

Simply put, it wasn't so much their difficulty that made the difference in their lives. It was their responses to the difficulty. The alcoholic twin blamed his failure on his father. He used that difficulty as an excuse for his lack of achievement. His brother, however, used the same difficulty as the motivating factor in his success.

The next step toward breaking the blame habit is to forgive. It is often difficult to forgive someone, especially when the other person doesn't deserve your forgiveness, doesn't even seek it, or is clearly in the wrong. But that's what the second twin learned to do. He learned to forgive.

Part of the difficulty comes from a common misunderstanding of what forgiveness is. Forgiving someone doesn't mean that the other person's behavior is okay. And it doesn't mean that the other person is off the hook. He's still responsible for his misbehavior.

Forgiveness is about letting yourself off the emotional blame hook. It's about releasing your negative emotions, attitudes, and behaviors, and letting go of the past so you can go forward to the future.

Then you can take the third step toward refusing to blame and accept responsibility for your feelings. Sooner or later, everyone you know will disappoint you in some way. They'll say something that will hurt you. Or they'll do something that will cause you to fail in some way. Hurt and disappointment are inevitable.

But you make things worse when you stew over someone's words and deeds. When you dwell on someone's rude remark or insensitive action, you're headed for deeper problems.

In fact, the more you dwell on those things, the more bitter you'll get. You'll find your joy, peace, and happiness slipping away. And you'll find your productivity slowing down as you spend more and more time thinking or talking about how you've been slighted. Eventually, if you don't stop doing this, you'll even get sick. Blame has a price.

So what should you do the next time someone betrays you? Learn to respond rather than react. Take responsibility for your feelings. Even though the other person may be at fault, even though the other person has wronged you, you are still responsible for your own feelings—because you *chose* your feelings.

Quite simply, other people do not and cannot cause your feelings. You choose them. For example, two people could be told that the suggestions they made at the staff meeting were stupid and idiotic. One person may choose to feel so hurt that he never speaks up at any other meeting again. The other person may choose to feel sorry for her critics, who couldn't see the wisdom and necessity of her suggestions.

As long as you blame other people for your feelings, as long as you believe other people have caused your feelings, you're stuck. You're a helpless victim.

But if you recognize the fact that you choose your feelings and you are responsible for your feelings, there's hope. You can take some time to think about your feelings. And you can decide what the best thing to say or do is in your particular situation. You can stay in charge.

If you're going to have a positive attitude, you must not blame anyone or anything for your failures. That's what losers do, and that's why they continue to be losers. As long as they can blame someone or something for their problems, they never do anything about them.

So be very careful when it comes to blame. Blame doesn't change anything. It doesn't make anything better. All blame can do is keep you stuck or make you spiteful, neither of which will build your positive attitude.

2. WHEN FAILURE COMES, STAY CALM

Many people tend to panic in the face of failure. And their positive attitudes seem to fizzle away. But this is an unproductive reaction that won't help you move beyond the setback. When failure comes, stay calm. Tell yourself that you're in charge, not your failure or your fear.

Unfortunately, for many people, panic comes all too easily. Panic is very dangerous. When you panic, you can't think straight, and you may not choose the right action to take. So stay calm—even though you may not necessarily *feel* calm. Behave with poise and composure. If you do, you'll receive three wonderful gifts.

First, you'll receive the gift of perspective. Calmness allows you to see things differently. The nineteenth-century American author

Ella Wheeler Wilcox knew that. She wrote, "The world is round, and the place that seems like the end may only be the beginning."

I'm sure you've experienced a failure that you initially thought was horrible. And then you found out that it was the best thing that could have happened to you. Or at least you found out that all things worked together for good. Your perspective made the difference.

The famous artist Pierre-Auguste Renoir learned that. He could have panicked during the last years of his life, when he was home-bound, almost paralyzed by arthritis.

The younger artist Henri Matisse was amazed that Renoir continued to paint. Finally he blurted out, "Auguste, why do you continue to paint when you are in such agony?"

Renoir's reply was simple and direct. He said, "The beauty remains; the pain passes."

How profound! By staying calm, Renoir was able to see what was most important. He was able to maintain his positive attitude. And he was able to keep on despite his arthritic setback.

Second, you'll receive the gift of wisdom. When you are calm you get a clearer idea as to what you should do next.

On a freezing night in December of 1914, Thomas Edison remained calm in the face of a setback when many others would have panicked and folded.

At the time, he was financially strapped as he worked to build a storage battery, a ten-year project. Then someone shouted, "Fire," and within moments his entire manufacturing plant was in flames. Fire departments came from eight towns, but the heat was so intense and the water pressure so low they could not put out the flames.

When Edison's son couldn't find his father, he was concerned. Was he safe? With all of his assets destroyed, would his spirit be broken?

Soon he saw his father running towards him. "Where's Mom?" shouted Edison. "Go get her, son. Tell her to hurry up and bring her friends. They'll never see a fire like this again."

The next morning, Edison called all of his employees together and made an incredible statement. He said, "We're rebuilding." He told one man to lease all the machine shops in the area. He told another one to get a wrecking crane. Then, as an after-thought, he asked, "Oh, by the way, anybody here know where we can get some money?"

Later Edison explained, "We can always make capital out of a disaster. We've just cleared out a bunch of old rubbish. We'll build bigger and better on the ruins." Then he yawned, rolled up his coat for a pillow, curled up on a table, and immediately fell asleep.

Edison stayed calm. I'm sure he had some feelings of disappointment and discouragement. That seems fairly normal. But he didn't let his negative feelings take over. He stayed calm. He kept his positive attitude, and that gave him the wisdom he needed to take the next step.

Could the same thing be said about you? Do you stay calm in the midst of failure? Do you keep your perspective, and do you get the wisdom you need?

If so, you'll also receive the third gift, the gift of persistence. You'll keep on doing what you need to do.

One day in the 1700s, as the Connecticut State Legislature was in session, it became ominously dark around noon. The sun was blotted out and stayed that way for some time. The Lower House adjourned in disorder, believing the world was coming to an end.

The Senate was more orderly because Senator Abraham Daven-port stayed calm. He arose to address his colleagues, saying, "If it is not the end of the world, we do not need to adjourn. If it is the end of the world, I would rather be here doing my duty when God finds me. I move that candles be brought and that we go on with our business."

And they did. Calmness gave them persistence. It gave them the ability to keep on doing what they needed to do.

The next time you feel like giving up or walking, stop yourself. Practice staying calm. If you have to force yourself to stay calm, do so. Calmness allows you to keep your positive attitude, and calmness makes it possible for you to work through your failure.

3. DO THE THING YOU FEAR

When you fail, you may be afraid of trying again. You may be afraid of additional failure, pain, and expense. Or you may be afraid of looking foolish or wasting your time.

Fear is similar to blame in the problems it creates. It keeps you stuck. You don't get past the failure. You simply remain fearful, and your positive attitude fizzles away.

The best strategy for getting past your fear and failure is to do the thing you fear. In other words, put the emphasis on action rather than denial. Instead of pretending you're not afraid, instead of telling yourself you're not afraid, do something about it.

Stand up to your fears. Tell yourself, "Yes, I'm afraid. I'm afraid of failing again. But I will not give in to this fear. I will not let it dominate my life." Then go out there and do the thing you fear. That's how you make the fear go away.

I know from my speaking experience that action is the only way to get around fear. I've given thousands of programs across the world, and I love it. But there was a time years ago when the fear of public speaking got in my way. So I practiced in front of my cats. You have to be very dramatic and animated to keep them mesmerized. If you don't, they'll just get up and walk off. I learned that if I can capture the attention of cats, then I can capture the attention of people. And my fear of public speaking subsided through my actions.

The late Supreme Court Justice William O. Douglas wrote about taking action to beat fear in his book, *Of Men and Mountains*. As a small boy, while lying beside a pool, he was thrown into the deep end by the school bully. He had never learned to swim and began to sink. He went down once, twice, and then someone pulled him out.

This terrifying experience caused him to fear water much of his life. His fear plagued him constantly. But then one day Douglas walked to the lakeshore. He looked at the water and felt the old terror once again. But instead of moving away from the water, he said, "With the help of God, I am now going to destroy this fear. The fear is here, but so is God." He plunged in, and it wasn't long before he learned to swim.

Do the thing you fear and the fear will go away. You'll move past the failure, and you'll have a stronger, more positive attitude to boot.

4. APPROACH EVERY FAILURE AS A LEARNING EXPERIENCE

When you experience failure, you can do several things. I've already talked about blaming, panicking, and giving up. You could also resolve to never again make another mistake, which is fine, but impractical. Or you could refuse to take any more risks that might not work out, which is foolish.

People with positive attitudes make up their minds to learn from their mistakes, which is the choice I advocate. True leaders and truly successful people don't give up when times get tough. When a day has gone badly or a piece of work has fallen apart, they stop to learn—and then they focus on the next time.

As a businessman, Arthur Gordon made a lot of money climbing the ladder of success. And then he made a number of bad decisions, resulting in the loss of his wife, kids, health, and money. He bottomed out. He became so depressed that he contemplated suicide.

Before he took such a drastic action, however, Arthur decided to consult the greatest psychiatrist in the United States. The psychiatrist was a well-respected eighty-year-old fellow who still maintained his practice.

Arthur talked about all of his problems. He told the psychiatrist about his bad decisions, his poor judgments, and the loss of his family and funds. Arthur went on for about fifteen minutes, explaining why life wasn't worth living anymore.

All of a sudden the old psychiatrist said, "That's enough. In the last fifteen minutes you've said the same phrase over and over again, and as long as you keep saying that phrase you will never get better. You keep using the two saddest words in the English language."

Arthur was curious. He wondered what the old psychiatrist meant.

The psychiatrist went on. "Those two words are 'If only.' You'd be amazed if you knew how many years I've sat in this chair and listened to thousands of people use those two words. They go on and on, starting all their sentences using those two words, until I finally stop them. I say to them, 'If only you would stop saying "if only," we might be able to get somewhere.'"

"What's the answer?" Arthur wanted to know. "What do you do?"

The psychiatrist said very simply, "You strike those two words from your vocabulary. And you substitute the two most powerful, positive words in the English language. You say, 'Next time.' This phrase faces you in the right direction, pulls you forward, and gives you lift instead of drag."

This psychiatrist's advice wasn't deep, complex, or theoretical. It was as simple as taking the time to learn from your failure—and then focus on the "next time."

Positive thinkers and winners do this all the time. They view every failure as a chance to learn. They believe that growth and learning can come from any situation, experience, problem, or crisis. So they're not deflated by the failures that come their way.

Could the same thing be said about you? Do you squeeze the lessons out of your failures? Do you focus on the "next times" of the future? Or do you dwell on the "if onlys" of the past?

Good doctors take this "next time" approach. Think about it. What would a doctor do if she called a sick patient into her examination room, but a few minutes later, the patient died? Would she quit? Would she take the rest of the day off because it wasn't going very well? No. She would do everything she could do to console the family, but after that she would focus her attention on the next patient that needed her.

The same goes for inventors. They approach every attempt and every failure as a step in a learning process that will eventually lead them to success. As Charles Kettering, one of the greatest inventors of the twentieth century, said, "An inventor fails 999 times, and if he succeeds once, he's in. He treats his failures simply as practice shots."

By treating failure as a learning experience, winners get better and better. They make fewer and fewer mistakes, and they reach future successes more and more quickly. As Earl Wilson said, "Experience is what enables you to recognize a mistake when you make it again."

In a sense, winners use failure as a map to point out dead ends and blind alleys. Thomas Edison did that as he worked on the invention of the electric light bulb. After some ten thousand experiments and no workable bulb, a reporter asked him how he felt about failing ten thousand times. He said, "I have not failed ten thousand times. I have successfully found ten thousand ways not to do it." Edison knew that a mistake was nothing more than feedback. He was learning a way not to do something.

You need to approach failure the same way. You need to see it as a learning experience. Remind yourself that the only time you really fail is when you make a mistake and do not learn from it.

Use your failure as a compass. Let it tell you where to go and not to go. Let it point you in the right direction. After all, as the Buddhists say, "If you are facing in the right direction, all you need to do is keep on walking."

So let failure be your teacher, not your master. And if you do, you'll be able to maintain your positive attitude in the most difficult of circumstances.

5. REMEMBER THE PROBLEM IS NOT THE PROBLEM

You may be wondering what "the problem is not the problem" means. In simple terms, it means "slow down." Don't jump to conclusions. Don't assume that your situation is the real problem. The real problem is how you see your situation.

Take, for example, a company reorganization. Two employees, working side by side, doing the same kind of work, can see the reorganization quite differently. One person can see it as a smart move that will make the company more competitive in the marketplace. The other person can see it as a major hassle that's not worth the effort. The real problem—or opportunity—is in how each of these people sees the situation.

The same is true in your personal life. Perhaps your children grow up and leave home. Some of you are saying, "Great. That's no problem." While others of you are saying, "That really hurts." The problem is not the problem. It's all in how you see your problem.

Unfortunately, we don't always see things clearly or correctly. That was the case when I met a longtime friend for lunch. He told me he needed to share a concern, that he thought his wife was pregnant with twins.

Knowing that he already had four children and his income was very low, I immediately expressed my concern as well. I said, "I can understand. Kids are so expensive these days. How could you possibly afford two more?"

My friend said, "That's not it at all. My concern is whether I'll have enough time to devote to each child so each one feels special."

How we see a situation makes all the difference in the world. I looked at my friend's situation as an economic challenge and would have immediately focused my energy on solving that economic "problem." My friend saw it as a life balance issue and started to look at how he might better manage his time.

So how do you see a situation clearly or correctly? How do you make sure that you don't turn a failure into a disaster? How do make sure you don't turn a stressful situation into a crisis? How do you stop yourself from turning a molehill into a mountain? You can begin by asking yourself the following four questions.

First, *does the situation really matter to me?* Your answer should be a simple yes or no, and it should be your yes or no. Don't let somebody else give you a guilt trip, or manipulate you into thinking you should care more than you do about the situation.

For example, if a person criticizes you and says, "You seem to be suffering from insanity," you don't have to let the criticism bother you. I know one person who would respond by saying, "No, I'm actually enjoying it more than ever."

Sometimes a situation just doesn't matter. One speaker I know of, John Hagee, is a very large man, and he's been criticized for his weight problem. But he just jokes it off by saying he qualifies for group insurance all by himself.

Second, *in the grand scheme of things, how big of a deal is it?* Does your situation qualify as a true catastrophe? Or will it be a lot less important in a day, a week, a month, or a year?

Maybe you're arguing with your spouse over which restaurant you'll choose, or maybe you're stressed out over the inadequate service at the restaurant. In the grand scheme of things, how big of a deal is it? Many people in the world spend their days trying to find food, while we spend our days trying to work it off.

To a great extent, your problems only have the size and the power you give them. If you exaggerate the severity of your problem, you could end up defeating yourself as well as killing off your positive attitude.

That's what comedian Rodney Dangerfield found out. He told his psychiatrist, "Everyone hates me." His psychiatrist said, "Don't be ridiculous. Everyone hasn't met you yet."

Third, *am I taking it personally?* Sometimes a prospective customer says no, but it has nothing to do with you or your product. The rejection isn't personal. It may just be bad timing. Sometimes your kid says no, but she would have said no to anybody or anything. She was just in a bad mood, and it had nothing to do with you.

So be careful; don't automatically assume you're to blame, and don't automatically take it personally. That's what one woman did when the Food and Drug Administration banned a certain medicine because it was habit forming. She said, "It's not habit forming. I ought to know. I've been taking it every day for the past nine years."

Fourth, *if I react now, will it make things better or worse?* Some things are better nipped in the bud while other things are better left alone for awhile.

Don't fall back on some self-justifying excuse, saying, "I jump in and deal with things immediately," or "I'm the type that lets things simmer for a while." Forget about the type you are or the things you always do. Focus on what works. Will you make things better or worse by reacting now?

Sometimes you have wonderful instincts, and you don't need a lot of time to think. Your first reaction is correct. For example, a recent study shows that 75 percent of the body's heat escapes through the head. Does that mean you could ski naked if you had a good hat? Your instincts should tell you that would be stupid.

Other times it makes more sense to think it through and then react. In fact, that's the case most of the time. As one man said after thinking through his financial failures, "I make money the old-fashioned way, but I spend it the modern way."

Ask yourself these four questions the next time you're faced with a problem. You'll see that the problem is not the problem. You'll see that your response to the problem is what really counts.

Psychologists call this "reframing." In other words, if you can redefine your failure in more positive terms, you won't lose your motivation or positive attitude. That's what Bobby Layne, the former pro football player with the Detroit Lions, found out. He said he never lost a game, he just ran out of time.

Perhaps the best reframing of failure comes from Robert Schuller. In his book, *Living Positively One Day at a Time*, Schuller described his thoughts on failure:

> Failure doesn't mean you're a failure. It means you haven't succeeded yet. Failure doesn't mean you have accomplished nothing. It means you have learned something. Failure doesn't mean you are a fool. It means you have a lot of faith.

Failure doesn't mean you've been disgraced. It means you were willing to try. Failure doesn't mean you don't have it. It means you must do it differently. Failure doesn't mean you are inferior. It means you are not perfect. Failure doesn't mean you wasted your life. It means you can start over.

Failure doesn't mean you ought to give up. It means you must try harder. Failure doesn't mean you never made it. It means it'll take longer. Failure doesn't mean God has abandoned you. It means he has a better idea.

Schuller's words are powerful. Whenever you fail, you need to remember the problem is not the problem. You need to reframe it in more positive terms—and then it will motivate you.

6. STEP OUT WITH DETERMINATION

A while ago, at one of my seminars, an audience member asked why some people succeed while others fail. Then she gave several examples of unlikely people succeeding and likely people failing.

She was one of the unlikely people who had succeeded in life. She was one of nine children born into a poverty-stricken family that was verbally, physically, and sexually abusive. She said that she was now the vice president of a corporation, with a substantial income and happily married. By contrast, all her siblings had gone through numerous jobs, marriages, and courtrooms, and none of them were even close to being successful at anything.

The class and I exchanged several ideas as to why some succeed and others fail. We talked about why some people hit bottom and stay there, while others bounce back to higher levels of success. We decided that the bounce-back winners keep their positive attitudes intact, and as a result, they are determined to go on.

I see it over and over again. Some people will tell me that they never had a chance to succeed. They are the wrong race, sex, or age, or they had the wrong parenting, schooling, or managing. But other people, of the same race, sex, or age, or with similar parenting, schooling, and managing, are doing quite well.

The difference is in their determination. Donald Bennett showed us that. A successful Seattle businessman and amputee, he had always wanted to climb Mt. Rainier. The mountain was so enticing, so beautiful, but very few ever climb it because the weather makes it impossible most of the time.

Donald trained and trained until he was given permission to climb the 14,410-foot-high mountain. The time eventually came, and he climbed 14,000 feet. But the weather forced him to turn back, which meant he had to wait another year. He had failed.

Many people would be too disappointed to try again, and they would quit. After all, they had given it a try, but it just didn't work out.

Not Donald. A year later, Donald Bennett stood on the top of Mt. Rainier on his one leg. He was the first amputee to make it to the summit. When a reporter asked him how he did it, Donald said, "One hop at a time." He was determined to be determined.

How do you get and keep that kind of determination? How do you maintain your determined positive attitude in the midst of failure? You can do three things.

First, *decide to be determined*. Abraham Lincoln said, "Always bear in mind that your own resolution to success is more important than any other one thing."

Determination is an intellectual thing. You decide to be determined even if you don't feel like it. You decide to be determined despite your disappointment and discouragement. You decide to keep your feelings in check. You know that your feelings provide useful information, but they are not allowed to have the final say in doing what you know you should be doing.

That's how Muhammad Ali became great. He even said, "I hated every minute of the training, but I said, 'Don't quit. Suffer now and live the rest of your life as a champion.'"

That was also the case with Fritz Kreisler. As a young boy he wanted to play the violin, and later he wanted a musical career. But it didn't work out the way he wanted, so he quit.

Kreisler decided to study medicine. He failed miserably at that. So he quit. He joined the army but never made it beyond the low rank of private. He quit again. He continued his pattern of trying different things and quitting each one of them.

Finally Kreisler went back to his former music teacher. He was told, "What you must have is the invincible, undefeatable determination that you will never give up." Kreisler took the advice to heart. He persevered until he finally succeeded. In fact, he became a world-famous violinist who would pack Carnegie Hall to capacity and keep his audiences spellbound.

Kreisler learned, as we all must learn, that in all worthwhile endeavors you must be prepared to endure before you can prevail. You must decide to be determined.

Second, you must *do your road work*. That's what Joe Frazier called it. As a young boy, Joe dreamed of becoming a boxer. He got an old sack and filled it with sand. That was his punching bag. And that was the beginning of his disciplined plan to achieve the success he wanted. Eventually he won the gold medal for boxing at the 1964 Olympic Games.

When asked about his secret, he said that success depends on your road work—or your practice and preparation. You must be willing to do your road work, week after week, month after month, and hurdle after hurdle. You can get anywhere you want to go if you are willing to keep at it—especially in times of failure.

Of course, at times you won't feel like doing your road work. I feel the same on occasion. But as I've said before, be wary of your feelings. They can be a useful guide in decision making, but they should never have the final say in doing what needs to be done.

The way I keep myself from giving up is to give myself an affirmation. I just repeat the following sentence over and over: "Never let up when you're ahead; never give up when you're behind." It works. It adjusts my attitude and gets me back to doing what I need to do.

Third, *refuse to let up*. Tom Dempsey was one person who refused to let up, despite his failures and limitations.

Tom was born with half a right foot and a deformed right arm and hand. And even though he played football in high school and college quite successfully, he was turned down by the professional teams. They looked at his disabilities and concluded he wasn't professional material.

Tom refused to accept their verdict. He said, "I have learned never to give up. So many times in life and in sports, I have seen things turn around because someone persevered and kept the faith." And so he kept the faith and made it into the big leagues.

In 1970, in a game between the Detroit Lions and the New Orleans Saints, the Saints were about to upset the Lions. With only eleven seconds left, Detroit took the lead by one point. It looked like the game was over. The Saints were on the forty-five-yard line with two seconds left. In came Tom Dempsey to kick a field goal.

Up to that time, the longest field goal had been fifty-six yards. This one would have to be sixty-three yards. The goal posts were so far away that Tom didn't even know he had made it until the official raised his arms. The Saints won because Tom Dempsey had refused to let up in life.

So you've failed a few times in life. Who hasn't? You've got to step out with determination anyway. When you feel like quitting, follow Winston Churchill's advice: "Never give up! Never, never give up!" It will do wonders for your attitude and your success.

Character Wins

Failure is not a case of *if*, but a case of *when*. And those who do the best in times of failure have learned to use the techniques from this chapter. They've learned to shake it off and step up.

Like the farmer who had an old mule who fell into a deep dry well. As he assessed the situation, he knew it would be difficult, if not impossible, to lift the heavy mule out of the deep well.

So the farmer decided to bury the mule in the well. After all, the mule was old and the well was dry, so he could solve two problems at once. He could put the old mule out of his misery and have his well filled.

The farmer asked his neighbors to help him with the shoveling. To work they went. As they threw dirt on the mule's back, the mule became frightened.

Then all of a sudden the mule got an idea. Each time they threw a shovelful of dirt on his back, he would shake it off and step up. Shovelful after shovelful, the mule would shake it off and step up. In not too long of a time, the exhausted and dirty mule stepped over the top of the well and through the crowd.

Like that mule, you need to shake off your failures. It will build your character, and it will nourish your attitude. As James Michener said, "Character consists of what you do on the third and fourth tries." And Martin Luther King, Jr., said, "The measure of a man is not where he stands in moments of comfort and convenience, but where he stands in times of challenge and controversy." Now it's your time to stand!

FAILURE EXERCISES

As we discussed earlier in this chapter, reframing is a process of re-defining a personal failure in such a way that the positive aspects of the failure are emphasized. Reframing is *not* rationalizing. When you rationalize, you try to justify your failure. And reframing is *not* denial. When you deny a failure, you refuse to think about it or deal with it.

Typically, when you make a mistake or fail at some task, you will do one of several nonproductive things. You may put yourself down, make up excuses for the failure, or pretend it never happened. None of them bring about positive results, however. In reframing, you stop yourself from acting out any of the above behaviors. You immediately admit your mistake or failure. You take responsibility for it—but you add a positive twist.

There are several ways you can reframe a "failure." Take a look at this example of reframing a computer error you made.

1. New Thought Approaches

a. Change your interpretation. ("I'm not stupid or incompetent. I simply got distracted and wasn't thinking.")

b. Minimize the negative. ("This is not like me. I have never made a mistake like this before.")

c. Use the negative. ("I will use my mistake as an example to teach my staff what not to do.")

2. New Behavior Approaches

a. Fix the negative. ("I'll stay calm, stay after work, and make the corrections.")

b. Plan future behavior. ("Next time I'll make sure I leave enough time at the end to double-check my work.")

c. Get help. ("It's more important to get the situation corrected than pretend I know it all. So it's okay to get some outside help.")

3. Getting Some Practice

a. Write down a recent mistake you made or failure you experienced that gave you a significant amount of stress.

b. What did you tell yourself when you made the mistake? In particular, how did you put yourself down or give yourself more stress?

c. What could you have said that would have been a *change in your interpretation*?

d. What could you have said that would have allowed you to *minimize the negative*?

e. What could you have said that would have *used the negative*?

f. How could you have *fixed the negative*?

g. How could you have *planned for future behavior*?

h. Where could you have *gone for help*?

A Final Note

To a great extent, your success or failure, your happiness or unhappiness, and even your health or lack of it is connected to your attitudes. The same goes for your self-esteem, relationships, enthusiasm, worry, and failure. So it might said, without too much exaggeration, that it's all about attitude. Certainly that's what you would hear from Dr. Charles Swindoll:

> The longer I live, the more I realize the impact of attitude on life. Attitude, to me, is more important than facts. It is more important than the past, than education, than money, than circumstances, than failure, than successes, than what other people think or say or do. It is more important than appearance, giftedness, or skill. It will make or break a company . . . a church . . . a home. The remarkable thing is we have a choice every day regarding the attitude we will embrace for that day. We cannot change our past. We

cannot change the fact that people will act in a certain way. We cannot change the inevitable. The only thing we can do is play on the one thing we have, and that is our attitude. I am convinced that life is 10 percent what happens to me and 90 percent how I react to it. And so it is with you. We are in charge of our attitudes.

Now that you know all of this, it's time for a revolution in your attitude. I urge you to reread and study the material in these chapters, and I challenge you to practice the attitude-building skills until you've mastered them. You're going to be absolutely delighted with the results you're going to get. I guarantee it!